THE
DISLOYAL
COMPANY

Transcontinental Books
1100 René-Lévesque Boulevard West
24th floor
Montreal (Quebec) H3B 4X9
Tel.: 514 340-3587
Toll-free 1 866 800-2500
www.livres.transcontinental.ca

Library and Archives Canada cataloguing in publication
Main entry under title:
The disloyal company: customers want to be loyal, but companies drive them away.

Includes bibliographical references.

ISBN 978-0-9809924-7-2

1. Marketing. 2. Customer relations. 3. Customer loyalty programs. 4. Marketing - Québec (Province). I. Leger Marketing.

HF5415.D57 2009   658.8   C2009-941695-6

Copy Editing: Trish O'Reilly
Proofreading: Marjorie Dunham-Landry
Page design: Diane Marquette, Transcontinental Books
Cover design: Studio Andrée Robillard

Printed in Canada
© Transcontinental Books, 2009
Legal deposit — 3rd quarter 2009
National Library of Quebec
National Library of Canada

We acknowledge the financial support of the Government of Canada through the Book Publishing Industry Development Program (BPIDP) and the Government of Quebec through the SODEC Tax Credit for our publishing activities.

For information on special rates for corporate libraries and wholesale purchases, please call **1 866 800-2500**.

THE
DISLOYAL
COMPANY

ACKNOWLEDGEMENTS

Since its creation in 1986, Leger Marketing has made a name for itself with the quality of its research and, above all, its inclination to bring together market research and polling practitioners and academics.

It is within this perspective that Leger Marketing created an Academic Committee made up of leading experts from various Canadian universities.

Members of this committee actively participated in the writing of this book, assisted by research professionals from Leger Marketing, in order to present to you the latest marketing discoveries.

Thank you to members of Leger Marketing's Academic Committee: Chuck Chakrapani, PhD (Ryerson University); Guy Lachapelle, PhD (Concordia University); Alan C. Middleton, PhD (Schulich School of Business, York University); Douglas Olsen, PhD (Arizona State University); and Sylvain Sénécal, PhD (HEC Montréal). Thanks also to Solange Tremblay (MA, Université du Québec à Montréal).

I would also like to thank my colleagues Christian Bourque, VP, Research; Dave Scholz, VP, Toronto; Dimitra Maniatis, Assistant VP, Toronto; and Arancha Pedraz-Delhaes, Project Director — all at Leger Marketing.

I owe a special thank you to Serge Lafrance, VP, Marketing, at Leger Marketing, who coordinated the various contributors.

Finally, we owe this book to all the disloyal companies that have inspired us and without which it could not have been written!

Jean-Marc Léger
President, Leger Marketing

TABLE OF CONTENTS

5

INTRODUCTION

There is only one boss. The customer. And he can fire anybody in the company from the Chairman on down, simply by spending his money somewhere else.

– Sam Walton, Walmart founder

The exponential growth in Internet use, the aging population, the balkanization of media, and the globalization of markets have changed the relationship between companies and clients: Power has changed hands. The consumer now has the power of life or death over a product, service, or business. We have moved from supply marketing to demand marketing. And the current economic crisis has only served to amplify this phenomenon.

Businesses must now navigate new paradoxes that make their relationships with consumers ever more complex:

• We are entering a digital era with an aging clientele.

• Market globalization is countered by client hyper-segmentation.

• Clients are over-leveraged, and overconsumption persists.

• We are a leisure society that lacks time.

When you face tomorrow's challenges with yesterday's methods, you end up with today's problems

A new consumer is emerging. This one is more sophisticated, more skeptical, more individualistic, more stressed for time, and more experienced — in short, more demanding of the products and services he or she consumes and the companies that offer them. Consumers have changed the way they think and, consequently, their way of spending. Our research has confirmed this:

▶ 91% of dissatisfied clients do not return.

▶ 96% of dissatisfied consumers do not file a complaint, which means that each complaint received corresponds to around 25 clients.

▶ On average, a dissatisfied client speaks to 13 people, while a satisfied client only speaks to 5 people.

▶ More than half of dissatisfied clients return if you correct your mistake, and 9 out of 10 will return if you correct it quickly.

Clients are not necessarily disloyal to companies, but companies are disloyal to clients!

The reality, however, goes beyond this. We have recently discovered that behind this dissatisfaction lies something even more fundamental that leads to consumer-company divorce: Consumers often feel betrayed by companies.

▶ 36% have felt betrayed by a company to whom they were loyal.

▶ 45% have felt that a company they were loyal to was treating new customers better than it was treating them.

▶ 70% of people believe that a majority of businesses care more about their profits than they do about their customers.

Contrary to what business leaders believe, clients are not necessarily disloyal to companies — but *companies are disloyal to clients!*

Disloyalty does not have a price; it only has consequences

One of the most significant examples of company disloyalty is that of cell phone providers, who offer free phones and three months of discounts to their new clients but, strangely enough, absolutely nothing to their regular, loyal clients.

Experiencing the same frustration are loyal supermarket customers who wait in line, their baskets full, while disloyal customers, flyers in hand, quickly go through the express cash with only a few price-reduced products.

Electronics are now being sold more often in superstores with a manufacturer's guarantee. If a problem occurs, however, the superstore does not provide service; in fact, sometimes it turns out that the store no longer even carries the product. It is often impossible, or simply too complicated, to contact the manufacturer. In the end, clients feel betrayed by both the superstore and the manufacturer.

It is no coincidence that companies in retail electronics, wireless services, credit cards, petroleum, and home improvement are perceived by consumers as being the most disloyal. (Inversely, the financial, pharmaceutical, and insurance sectors are perceived as being the least disloyal.)

The Leger Marketing Canadian Disloyalty Index: case studies

In this book, the leading researchers in Canada have studied this phenomenon, shedding new light on company disloyalty.

To begin with, we discuss examples of companies being disloyal to clients (Chapter 1), the roots of disloyalty and how it can be countered by prioritizing loyalty strategies (Chapter 2), and examples of "brand treachery" (Chapter 3). Chapter 4 provides examples of disloyal companies' irrational behaviour and reviews the findings of a survey that asked consumers about their feelings of betrayal.

In Chapter 5, we discuss how to measure company behaviour, and we present the Leger Marketing Canadian Disloyalty Index: a worst-to-best list of disloyal companies. And, to save you the trouble of flipping ahead to find out, some of the companies that scored the lowest on the Canadian Disloyalty Index are Air Transat, Air Canada, Bell Mobility, Future Shop, and Petro-Canada, while some of those that ranked highest are Manitoba Hydro, PC Financial, Scotiabank, Starbucks, and FedEx. The chapter gives a more detailed and comprehensive breakdown of the Canadian Disloyalty Index.

In Chapter 6, we explain how consumers are being empowered by the Internet. However, as we shall see, this growth in consumer power in no way helps disloyal or incompetent companies become less so. In conclusion, Chapter 7 offers a reflection on the "New Era of Sustainable Development and Responsible Organizations."

To get results you've never had, you've got to do what you've never done

This book will appeal to anyone who is interested in customer service, marketing, and communications. This includes company leaders, marketing and sales vice-presidents and directors, and managers in charge of quality control and communications. It will also appeal to investors, customers, and students who want to avoid blindly accepting the unfounded dogma of consumer disloyalty. Of course, we also highly recommend that all the disloyal companies mentioned in the chapters of this book purchase a copy for themselves!

Moreover, to those managers who are always asking themselves what they should be doing to satisfy clients, we invite them to ask themselves instead what they should *avoid* doing that is creating dissatisfied customers and driving them away. If they want to get results they've never had, they've got to do what they've never done. *That* is what this book proposes.

Jean-Marc Léger
President, Leger Marketing
August 2009

Chapter 1

THE DISLOYAL COMPANY — OR THE MYTH OF THE DISLOYAL CONSUMER

Serge Lafrance, Leger Marketing

Believing in Consumer Disloyalty

Today, the most effective assertion a speaker can make to pique the interest and win the approval of an audience of marketing or sales practitioners is that consumers are disloyal *and increasingly so*. This has been observed on several occasions during recent symposiums, conferences, and seminars addressed to marketers. And the stereotype is so pervasive that it has become accepted as a self-evident truth in marketing circles — an unshakeable belief that is never questioned and for which no one is ever asked to produce any hard evidence.

Unfortunately, being convinced of consumer disloyalty prompts marketing practitioners to behave in such a way that their actions actually lessen client loyalty, which then reinforces their belief that customers are disloyal. It is a vicious circle and results in disloyal clients often receiving better treatment from the company in question than loyal ones. This, of course, is absurd: Why would a company choose to alienate its most important core group of customers? One example of this phenomenon can be found in the telecommunications sector, where non-subscribers and former subscribers often receive tantalizing proposals, such as three months free of charges or free phones for all newcomers, leaving the current clientele out in the cold.

Natural Consumer Loyalty

However, one could come to the opposite conclusion: Consumers, when satisfied with their initial choice, tend to be naturally and fundamentally loyal. Moreover, they desperately want to sustain this loyalty because it has a number of advantages.

Three principles taken from consumer behaviour theory can serve as a foundation to explain the loyalty that consumers naturally seek:

Perceived risk: Consumers want to reduce risk, and it just so happens that loyalty is an effective way to eliminate it.

In fact, there is no risk with remaining loyal to a satisfactory choice, but being disloyal and choosing the unknown is risky, especially for products or services that involve moderate to major investment, such as a new brand of television or a new car.

Cognitive consistency — seeking common ground: Consumers find psychological comfort in behaving coherently and consistently with respect to what they know, think, and believe. Despite a vast choice of restaurants close to the office, there is something reassuring about always returning to the same one! A satisfactory experience with a place, brand, or company means that the same behaviour is adopted for subsequent purchases.

The need for consumers to facilitate and simplify their lives: Consumers achieve this by reducing the time devoted to purchasing decisions and the amount of information they must process in order to decide. For example, in the interests of making their lives easier, few consumers review all insurance companies when they renew their policies. Indeed, loyalty itself makes a decision easier, even if we know we're not getting the best price.

Reward the Loyal, Not the Disloyal

Think of the subscriber who has remained loyal to a television cable provider for 15 years. Each year, this consumer sees the provider offer significant services, bonuses, and other trimmings to non-subscribers and former disloyal subscribers, while he or she never receives anything special, even though payments have been made in full for the past 180 months of a long-standing business relationship. If this subscriber were to cancel the subscription, he or she would receive better treatment from the provider with an offer of free services to renew the subscription.

The same frustration is experienced by the loyal supermarket customer who waits in line with his or her basket full, while disloyal customers, flyers in hand, quickly go through the express cash with only a few price-reduced products. Another case is that of the loyal telephone company subscriber who hears former disloyal subscribers brag about the major incentives they received from the provider to reclaim them as clients. Rewarding the disloyal is a strange way of encouraging client loyalty!

The stereotypical belief that consumers are disloyal is unfounded. If consumers are sometimes disloyal, it is more often out of frustration than because they wish to be disloyal. In fact, marketing practitioners behave in a way that causes disloyalty. The rules must change to better serve clients. Presented here are three approaches — or "rules" — to address this problem.

Rule #1: Understand and Avoid Anti-Marketing

In marketing, the four P's (price, place, product, promotion) teach us what to do to serve our clients well, and the four anti-marketing I's (disrespect, inconsistency, indifference, incompetence) teach us what not to do to avoid losing them.

Disrespect

Not to be outdone by the telephone industry, the newspaper industry often uses the same approach. Here, new subscribers will receive two months of newspaper delivery to their homes at a preferential rate, whereas loyal subscribers receive little or nothing.

The insurance industry has a habit of contacting its clients once a year, when it's time to send the invoices renewing their insurance policies. This is the extent of their customer service and often the extent of any kind of contact. And, year after year, while the long-standing clients' premiums increase, discounts are often reserved for new policyholders.

Inconsistency

For years, automobile manufacturers have been offering leasing contracts on their vehicles. It is a nice initiative, but how do you explain the inconsistency of a business policy that penalizes (by as much as $1,000 to $3,000) a consumer who would like to exchange his or her vehicle (for the same, more recent, make with the same dealership) for the duration of the contract? Why is this penalty applied if the client wants the same brand of car at the same location?

Moreover, a further example of inconsistency can be seen at Mercedes, which now offers models for $25,000 — insulting for loyal consumers who, for the past 10 years, have been paying $130,000 for luxury models.

Indifference

How many times has a consumer at a service counter been confronted with a representative who, though apologetic, gives a telephone call priority and makes the customer wait? The client has made the effort to go in person to ensure the best possible service — only to be met with indifference. Car dealerships, banks, travel agencies, and government services all tend to perform at a rather high level on measures of indifference!

It seems that airports, on the other hand, have actually set international standards when it comes to indifference towards users: In airports across the world, we see the same duty-free shops, the same rest areas, and the same mediocre restaurants — in short, a common indifference towards customer service throughout the world.

Incompetence

Increasingly, consumer use of the Internet makes sales representatives look bad in various industries, particularly in the technology, telecommunications, and automotive sectors; with access to information online, consumers are often better informed than the sales representatives. This is certainly a major challenge for companies, but incompetence has no place in customer service.

Regardless of which industry you work in, the four anti-marketing I's lie in wait. A consumer never chooses to defect for no reason; he or she leaves because of dissatisfaction. And, more often than not, a consumer leaves because a company has failed in its promise to serve its clients well.

Rule #2: Always Think of Your Garage Mechanic!

Who doesn't dream of pledging lifelong loyalty to a trustworthy garage mechanic?

How many actually do it?

Excuses and more excuses...

Consumer disloyalty is a stereotype that suits marketing practitioners. It diverts them from their responsibilities as researchers and strategists and makes it easier for marketing and sales representatives or company management to blame poor quarterly or annual results on *disloyal clients*. "Competition is fierce, consumers are disloyal, and this is why we lost 10% of our market share." Or even: "This long-term client turned his back on us to do business with a competitor, without telling us and without reason."

Without reason? Really?

Loyalty is earned

Touting consumer disloyalty has become too shamefully easy. A more accurate — and, we admit, more provocative — affirmation would be to say that consumers desperately *want* to be loyal. Consumers are looking for companies that will keep their promise of a quality product or service, at a fair price, within a reasonable time frame, and without any breach of trust.

Imagine again a consumer's delight in having a reliable garage mechanic! By remaining loyal, the consumer knows that he or she gets better service. The consumer becomes a familiar face, entitled to personalized service and certain advantages when making appointments. Moreover, as trust is established, risk levels drop, and the consumer gets a fair price, which is not the case at all garages! The consumer who is loyal to a garage mechanic saves time, money, and stress. This consumer feels more at ease because returning to a known location has a comforting appeal.

When you find a garage mechanic who offers quality service at reasonable prices and wait times, you do not go elsewhere just for the sake of being disloyal. You want this garage mechanic to maintain service quality. If promises are not kept, dissatisfaction, *not* intentional disloyalty, makes you look elsewhere.

So, the next time your sales director blames poor quarterly or annual results on client disloyalty, think of your garage mechanic.

Rule #3: If Your Clients Are Satisfied, Beware!

Satisfied clients can be counted on to some extent, but they can also be lulled into remaining *merely* satisfied. As in interpersonal relationships, the spark must be kept alive.

Satisfying your clients is not enough...

One story comes to mind that illustrates how satisfying a client can sometimes fall short. I asked a friend if he liked his golf instructor and the golf course he played on, and he answered, without any great excitement, that he was *satisfied*. I understood from this that his golf instructor was doing his work adequately and no more. I also understood that if this instructor had *surpassed* my friend's expectations, he would have heartily recommended him. The lesson learned is interesting. In business, we have long known that a *dissatisfied* client does not help a company's cause, but a *satisfied* client may not contribute much to business development either. If you want satisfied clients to act as business drivers for the company, you have to know how to surprise them. Clients should want to recommend you, talk about you, and sing the praises of your products and services. Certainly, satisfying your customers begins with meeting their expectations. But if your objective is only to satisfy your clients, you need to remind yourself that this is not enough.

The real challenge — the unexpected

Satisfaction is a state that lasts only a short time, such as the momentary feeling you get after consuming a pleasant breakfast. In fact, once you have eaten breakfast, the desire for lunch and supper soon follows. The same goes for customer satisfaction. Once they have what they want, customers almost immediately seek to meet other needs — a never-ending process. So a company will never get to the finish line and be able to say "That's it, my clients are happy now." Tomorrow, it starts all over again. How do you add to the satisfaction of clients who are already fulfilled? How do you offer Disneyland to someone who has already visited Disneyland? How do you succeed in improving services for clients who consider themselves more than satisfied? The only way to succeed is to continually improve and offer the unexpected.

Create modest expectations

No doubt, a friend has at some point suggested a small, unpretentious restaurant, saying "You'll see, you'll be surprised." For the restaurateur, this is a good opportunity to surpass your expectations and impress you.

In general, creating high expectations is not a winning strategy. You run the risk of your clients being simply satisfied but not at all surprised or impressed. Moreover, you establish a precedent for quality and service that you will have to surpass the next time. If you think it through, it is better to create lower expectations you are sure to reach — and then surpass them. In fact, many companies listed on the stock exchange have been successfully using the "under-promise and over-deliver" approach for years. They create modest but realistic expectations for their financial results, knowing full well that at the end of each quarter, they will be able to congratulate themselves on the better-than-expected re-sults. The key to success is knowing how to manage expectations.

Your clients, even those who are satisfied, will not necessarily contribute to your enterprise's development. To do that, in addition to being satis-fied, your clients must want to recommend and stay with your company. Only then will you be able to say that you have loyal customers because of your own loyalty to them.

BIBLIOGRAPHY

Lafrance, Serge, and Robert Desormeaux. 2001. "Le mythe de l'infidélité des consommateurs." *Gestion* 26 (3) (fall).

Lafrance, Serge, and Jean-Marc Léger. 2005. "L'antimarketing." *Commerce* (July).

Lafrance, Serge, and Jean-Marc Léger. 2008. "Comment tuer une marque." *Commerce* (September).

Lafrance, Serge, and Jean-Marc Léger. 2005. "L'entreprise infidèle." *Commerce* (November).

Lafrance, Serge, and Jean-Marc Léger. 2003. "Imitez votre garagiste." *Commerce* (July).

Lafrance, Serge, and Jean-Marc Léger. 2004. "Vos clients sont satisfaits? Méfiez-vous!" *Commerce* (May).

Chapter 2

THE ROOTS OF DISLOYALTY AND SOME STRATEGIES TO BUILD LOYALTY

Chuck Chakrapani, PhD, Ryerson University

Dave Scholz, Leger Marketing

Market Norms vs. Social Norms

Consumers accept most business transactions as a simple exchange between two parties: the company and the customer. The parties enter into transactions for personal benefits: The company gets economic benefits, and the consumer gets the product or service he or she needs. The company has the right to set the price and terms for its products and services, while the consumer has the right to accept or reject those terms.

Such business transactions are based on what are known as *market norms*. Market norms are not personal. In following market norms, the company attempts to optimize economic gains while the consumer attempts to optimize the benefits derived. Neither party is particularly interested in helping or hindering the other.

When transactions follow market norms, the company owes nothing to the consumer (except what is agreed upon and what would be considered reasonable); similarly, the consumer owes nothing to the company. As a result, the consumer is free to switch companies when he or she encounter, a better offer. When the transaction is purely business, there's no rationale for a consumer to continue to fly Airline A if he or she can get the same service at a lower cost from Airline B. The logic of market norms provides no enduring basis for customer loyalty in a business transaction. Other things being equal, there is no reason a customer should continue to patronize the same firm when a better offer is on the table.

This poses a problem for companies. Each transaction, in essence, becomes a new sale with attendant marketing costs.[1] Under these conditions, then, can a company persuade a customer to stay with it even though the deal offered may not be the best from a business perspective? Is there a way by which a company can entice a customer to go beyond *market norms*? Can a company persuade the customer to stay on, even though an apparently better deal is available elsewhere?

Research in social psychology and behavioural economics suggests that this can be achieved by shifting the framework from market norms to *social norms*, in which transactions are not precisely matched in terms of their economic value. A birthday present you bought for your friend may have cost you $80, and the present she bought for you may have cost $57. But this is a social transaction, and social norms are not economics-based — so no one is going to feel short-changed by this apparent inequity. In fact, in most cultures, it would be unacceptable even to evaluate the monetary worth of social transactions. Such social norms may be extended to company-customer relationships. A bank, for example, could state or imply that it intends to treat its loyal customers using social norms in a reciprocal way. This could mean many things to a customer: For instance, if the customer has been loyal to the company, some service charges could be overlooked; loans could be arranged faster; some rigid rules could be relaxed; and so on.

Trust and Loyalty

To better understand the relationship between what a company does and how it influences a consumer, we need to understand the role of consumer trust. "Trust" can be defined as a belief that an exchange partner is benevolent and honest (Doney, Cannon, and Mullen 1998; Geyskens, Steenkamp, and Kumar 1998). Consumer trust in the company confers many rewards for the company. Grayson, Johnson, and Chen (2008) identify how a company can increase customer loyalty (Augustin and Singh 2005) and commitment (Jap and Ganesan 2000), encourage greater usage (Maltz and Kohli 1996), and reduce consumer opportunism (Rindfleisch and Moorman 2003). The effect of trust is widespread and varied: It can affect the way consumers respond to the company's promotions (Hulme 2005), maximize the acceptance of advice provided by the representatives of a financial company (Starkman 2005), and even increase the likelihood that consumers will adopt vaccinations offered by a pharmaceutical company (Burton 2005). Because trust in a company positively influences consumer behaviour, such as loyalty, trust is an important component of company performance.

Both social norms and market norms can create trust, provided they are consistently followed. A problem is created, however, when a company adopts social norms because of their many benefits but reverts back to market norms when it is expected to engage in reciprocal behaviour.

This is clearly illustrated in an example studied by Gneezy and Rustichini (2000), as reported by Don Ariely (2008). A few years ago, a daycare facility in Israel introduced a monetary fine as a deterrent to parents who showed up late to pick up their children. The reasoning behind the fine was that if parents were forced to pay for their tardiness, they would show up on time to pick up their children. However, the strategy had exactly the opposite effect: Fewer parents picked up their children on time.

When there were no fines, parents felt guilty about making caregivers wait and tried to be on time as much as possible. However, once a fine was introduced for late pickups, they felt less guilty about being late because they were "paying" for their late arrival. What is even more interesting is this:.When the daycare centre noticed the ineffectiveness of levying a fine, it stopped the fine. Yet parents continued to arrive late — as late as when there were fines. In fact, there was a slight increase in late pickups now that no social norms were present *and* market norms imposed no penalty. As Ariely (2008) puts it, "when a social norm collides with a market norm, the social norm goes away for a long time." Thus, once social norms are replaced by market norms, it is very difficult to go back to social norms.

This has an obvious parallel for the business world. When companies adopt social norms and later revert to market norms, it can have a deleterious effect on consumer trust, which in turn can lead to "customer disloyalty."

Adopting Social Norms: Rewards and Perils

Since the 1980s, businesses have been gradually adopting social norms to make consumers act in the companies' interests and reaping all the benefits that flow from them. Even the words they use evoke social norms. It's not a "usage" card but a "loyalty" card. We are not waiting for an hour on the telephone because the company does not think our call is important enough to be promptly answered by a human being but because the company assures us that "your call is important to us." The telephone charges are not increased to benefit the firm but to provide you with "even better service." Financial institutions increase their hours of operation not to increase their profits but to provide better service to customers. Adopting social norms can be rewarding to companies, but it does not come free of obligations. When companies adopt (or are perceived to adopt) a social norm and later renege on it, they can inadvertently create disloyal customers. So, customer disloyalty can be seen as a reaction to company disloyalty.

Reframing market norms into social norms may work for a while, but not for long. The main reason for this is that social norms require reciprocation. If someone has been "loyal" to the company, he or she expects something in return because it is part of the implied social contract: If I look after your interests, I expect you to look after mine. This is the basis of social norms.

When a firm has a recorded message that says "Your call is important to us" and keeps the customer waiting for an hour, when a firm says it values employee loyalty but doesn't hesitate to get rid of a loyal employee because of "restructuring," when a firm provides more benefits to potential and new customers than to those who have been loyal, this implied contract is breached. And the breach of social norms leads to lack of trust. This lack of trust — which originates in company disloyalty — is often seen by the company as customer disloyalty.

Are the effects of faking social norms worse than the effects of simply using business norms? Current research shows that this is indeed so. When business norms prevail, customers may not be "loyal" to the firm, but the firm is not burdened further with customer distrust. However, when companies act as if they are following social norms as opposed to market norms and then don't live up to their end of the bargain (such as looking after customers' interests), customers will not only revert to business norms but be less trusting of the firms' business promises. Much of the above discussion is based on findings from social psychology. (For an example, see Cialdini 2009.) The position we take here is that much of customer disloyalty can be traced back to firm disloyalty to customers.

Both consumer loyalty and trust are negatively affected when a firm adopts social norms and then abandons them when it is in the firm's short-term interest to do so.

Method

To test these propositions directly, we analyzed some of the tactics used by prominent companies that have customer loyalty programs and often imply in their ads that they reward loyal customers or loyal employees. We further identified instances in which the same companies appear to breach social norms. We then created alternative hypothetical scenarios to test how people would react if the situations were handled differently. (While we don't identify the companies by name, the hypothetical scenarios are all based on real situations.) These parallel scenarios were evaluated by two different sets of respondents, with approximately 800 in each set for a total of over 1,600 in all. Based on the respondents' answers, we were able to evaluate the effects of the companies' tactics on consumer loyalty and consumer trust.

Strategies for Using Social Norms in a Business Context

Using social norms when the transactions are based on market norms poses some major problems. Social norms require not only reciprocity but also consistency. What happens when the business interests of a firm make it nearly impossible to conform to social norms? As we have seen, reverting to market norms once social norms have been projected actually makes matters worse because trust is broken (more on this later).

One strategy is to project only market norms. This is definitely a superior strategy to that of adopting social norms and later switching to market norms. The downside, however, is that while it is relatively easy to establish trust based on market norms, this approach does not necessarily build customer loyalty, especially in a competitive market. Further, since "customer satisfaction" and "customer loyalty" are being constantly touted in advertisements and through seals of endorsement like J.D. Power, many customers have begun to expect companies to operate according to social norms. However, companies can adopt some strategies that combine market and social norms so that customers will continue to trust them. In this chapter, we will discuss a few of these strategies with research findings to support them.

Strategy 1: Placing social norms in a business context

Application of social norms means that not every transaction between customers and the company has to be perfectly balanced in terms of value. This, of course, makes the adaptation of social norms attractive to businesses. However, applying social norms in a business context can sometimes be too expensive. Consider a situation in which a cell phone company offers new customers 20% off for the next 12 months. Should it give the same deal to all its current customers? Doing so would not make a lot of sense because this means subsidizing by 20% the entire customer database, the bulk of which may not even be aware of the special deal. If the company hopes to acquire 5% more customers through this deal, subsidizing the entire customer database would reduce the total revenue by 20%, which would not make business sense.

Is it possible to use business norms in this context without breaching social norms? To test this, we created two alternative scenarios. In the first scenario, the firm fails to acknowledge social norms and reverts to market norms when it is advantageous for it to do so. This scenario was presented to more than 800 respondents to determine its effect on loyalty and trust:

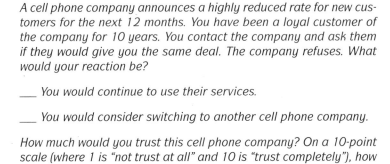

*A cell phone company announces a highly reduced rate for new cus-
tomers for the next 12 months. You have been a loyal customer of
the company for 10 years. You contact the company and ask them
if they would give you the same deal. The company refuses. What
would your reaction be?*

___ *You would continue to use their services.*

___ *You would consider switching to another cell phone company.*

*How much would you trust this cell phone company? On a 10-point
scale (where 1 is "not trust at all" and 10 is "trust completely"), how
would you rate this company?*

For another group of more than 800 respondents, we presented a second scenario. The alternative scenario is identical to the first in that the
firm does not accede to the request of the customer to provide the same
deal. However, in the second scenario, the firm uses business norms,
without breaching social norms:

*A cell phone company announces a highly reduced rate for new cus-
tomers for the next 12 months. You have been a loyal customer of
the company for 10 years. You contact the company and ask them
if they would give you the same deal. The company says that for
business reasons, it cannot do that. But since your business is valuable to the company, they agree to give you a better deal than what
you have now. What would your reaction be?*

___ *You would continue to use their services.*

___ *You would consider switching to another cell phone company.*

*How much would you trust this cell phone company? On a 10-point
scale (where 1 is "not trust at all" and 10 is "trust completely"), how
would you rate this company?*

The results proved interesting. When the social norm was taken into account, five times as many respondents (49%) said that they would continue to use the firm that acknowledged the social norm as opposed to
the firm that did not (10%). When the social norm was simply ignored,
81% of respondents said that they would consider switching to another

cell phone company. However, when the social norm was acknowledged in terms of some alternative benefit to the customer (not even specified in the scenario), only about 44% said that they would consider switching to another cell phone company. Even more important, its effect on the trust level was equally dramatic. As shown in Table 2.1, four times as many trusted the firm that acknowledged social norms compared to the one that didn't, by giving a rating of at least 7 on a 10-point scale.

_____ Table 2.1 _____

EFFECT OF ACKNOWLEDGING SOCIAL NORMS ON TRUST, CELL PHONE RATES SCENARIO

EFFECT ON TRUST	PERCENTAGE WHO TRUSTED	MEAN SCORE
When social norms were ignored	6%	3.1
When social norms were acknowledged	23%	4.6

Note: Means are from a 10-point scale where 1 = "not trust at all" and 10 = "trust completely."

_____ Figure 2.1 _____

EFFECT OF ACKNOWLEDGING SOCIAL NORMS ON LOYALTY, CELL PHONE RATES SCENARIO

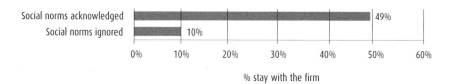

% stay with the firm

_____ Figure 2.2 _____

EFFECT OF ACKNOWLEDGING SOCIAL NORMS ON TRUST, CELL PHONE RATES SCENARIO

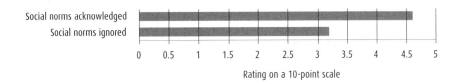

This finding suggests the first strategy for building loyalty and trust:

_____

Strategy 1: *If business realities make it difficult to hold to the social norm, it might be a better strategy to find a compromise between market norms and social norms than to abandon social norms completely.*

_____

Strategy 2: Reframing the offer to avoid breaching social norms

Another common strategy used by companies is to present their offering in only the most favourable terms. This tends to attract many new customers. An example of this would be the use of airline points. Some airlines advertise that you can fly to a given destination with a certain number of points. Yet most customers cannot get this deal because it is the best case scenario, available on a first come first served basis perhaps a year in advance. Since this aspect is not advertised, customers are not generally aware that the advertised deal has some implied hidden conditions. Customers who believe that they could get this deal find that, by and large, they cannot. Customers may well feel that they fulfilled their part of the social norm by being loyal to the airline, but the airline is not loyal to them in return by delivering on the promised flight. This also adversely affects the trust customers place in the company.

Could the company keep the loyalty and trust of customers by reframing its offer? To test this, we created two alternative scenarios. In the first scenario, the airline makes it difficult for customers to understand why they cannot get the reward promised by the airline when they agreed to be loyal. This scenario was presented to more than 800 respondents to determine its effect on loyalty and trust:

> *An airline announces that you can fly to the destination of your choice for 50,000 airline points. But no matter when you try to book a flight, it always seems to be unavailable. However, you learn that seats are available fairly easily if you have 150,000 points. You also learn that to get a flight for 50,000 points, you need to book your flight almost a year in advance. What would your reaction be?*
>
> ___ *You would continue to use the airline's services.*
>
> ___ *You would consider switching to another airline.*
>
> *How much would you trust this airline ? On a 10-point scale (where 1 is "not trust at all" and 10 is "trust completely"), how would you rate this airline?*

A second scenario was presented to another group of more than 800 respondents. This scenario offer is identical to the first one in terms of content. However, in the second scenario, the offer is reframed such that the offer more easily attained by the customer is presented first, along with information on how he or she can get a much better offer if he or she books well in advance.

> *An airline announces that you can fly to the destination of your choice for 150,000 airline points, which you think is too high. However, the airline informs you that if you book your flight almost a year in advance, you can fly to the same destination for as low as 50,000 points. What would your reaction be?*
>
> ___ *You would continue to use the airline's services.*
>
> ___ *You would consider switching to another airline.*

How much would you trust this airline? On a 10-point scale (where 1 is "not trust at all" and 10 is "trust completely"), how would you rate this airline?

By reframing the offer in terms of what customers can actually expect to get in return for their loyalty (rather than what they might get under unspecified special circumstances), the firm does not breach the social norm. Consequently, we expected the second scenario to be more appealing to respondents.

So what did we find? Four times (40%) as many respondents said they would continue with the program when the second scenario was presented compared to the first scenario (11%). Intention to switch, which was 75% for the first scenario, dropped substantially to 40% for the second.

More important, its effect on the trust level was dramatic. As Figure 2.2 shows, three times as many trusted the firm that was seen to honour social norms compared to the one that didn't seem to, by giving a rating of at least 7 on a 10-point scale.

_____ Table 2.2 _____

EFFECT OF ACKNOWLEDGING SOCIAL NORMS ON TRUST, AIRLINE POINTS SCENARIO

EFFECT ON TRUST	PERCENTAGE WHO TRUSTED	MEAN SCORE
When social norms were seen to be violated	6%	3.2
When social norms were seen to be upheld	19%	4.6

Note: Means are from a 10-point scale where 1 = "not trust at all" and 10 = "trust completely."

_____ Figure 2.3 _____

EFFECT OF ACKNOWLEDGING SOCIAL NORMS ON LOYALTY, AIRLINE POINTS SCENARIO

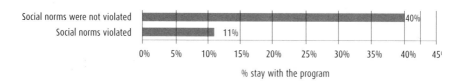

% stay with the program

_____ Figure 2.4 _____

EFFECT OF ACKNOWLEDGING SOCIAL NORMS ON TRUST, AIRLINE POINTS SCENARIO

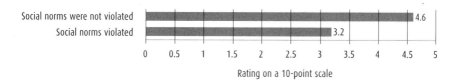

Rating on a 10-point scale

This finding suggests the second strategy for building loyalty and trust:

Strategy 2: If a firm makes it easy for customers to see that it honours social norms, customers are more likely to reciprocate by being loyal and keeping trust.

Strategy 3: Not emphasizing social norms

Yet another strategy to prevent customer erosion is to avoid using social norms if they can't be honoured. While there are many advantages to adopting them, social norms that are broken are far worse than business norms that are kept. We will illustrate this using the relationship between a firm and its employees.

In the first scenario, the firm projects social norms by making the employees believe that their loyalty will be valued. Employees keep their end of the bargain by being loyal to the company. Yet when the time comes, market norms dominate the decision of the firm and an employee is let go. This scenario was presented to more than 800 respondents to determine its effect on loyalty and trust:

> *A person who works with you has been with the company for many years. He has been told repeatedly that his loyalty is valued. The company decides to move some of its operations offshore and, in a purely business decision, lays off your colleague. What would your reaction be?*
>
> *___ You would continue to work there.*
>
> *___ You would onsider switching to another employer.*
>
> *How much would you trust your company? On a 10-point scale (where 1 is "not trust at all" and 10 is "trust completely"), how would you rate this company?*

In the second scenario, exactly the same situation is presented. An employee who has been with the company for many years is let go because it is in the interests of the business. The one exception is that the firm is run on market norms and does not pretend to subscribe to social norms.

> *A person who works with you has been with the company for many years. The company has always treated its employees fairly, but in a business-like fashion with no promises. The company decides to move some of its operations offshore and, in a purely business decision, lays off your colleague. What would your reaction be?*
>
> *___ You would continue to work there.*
>
> *___ You would consider switching to another employer.*
>
> *How much would you trust your company? On a 10-point scale (where 1 is "not trust at all" and 10 is "trust completely"), how would you rate this company?*

Our hypothesis here is that people are not upset by the market norm but by the representation of it as a social norm. If this hypothesis is correct, then erosion of loyalty and trust will be higher for the first scenario than for the second. Here is what we found.

Forty-eight percent of respondents said they would continue with the firm that projected the market norm, while only 28% said so about the firm that projected the social norm but later reneged on it.

The effect on the trust level is equally illuminating. As Table 2.3 shows, more than twice as many trusted the firm that did not use social norms merely as leverage to obtain loyalty compared to the one that did, by giving a rating of at least 7 on a 10-point scale.

Table 2.3

EFFECT OF ACKNOWLEDGING SOCIAL NORMS ON EMPLOYEE TRUST, LAYOFF SCENARIO

EFFECT ON TRUST	PERCENTAGE WHO TRUSTED	MEAN SCORE
When social norms were ignored	8%	3.4
When social norms were acknowledged	19%	4.4

Note: Means are from a 10-point scale where 1 = "not trust at all" and 10 = "trust completely."

Figure 2.5

EFFECT OF ACKNOWLEDGING SOCIAL NORMS ON EMPLOYEE LOYALTY, LAYOFF SCENARIO

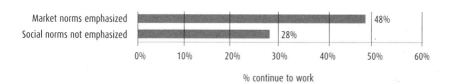

% continue to work

_____ Figure 2.6 _____

EFFECT OF ACKNOWLEDGING SOCIAL NORMS ON EMPLOYEE TRUST, LAYOFF SCENARIO

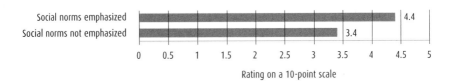

Rating on a 10-point scale

This leads to our third strategy:

Strategy 3: *When it is known that it is not possible to keep social norms on a long-term basis, or when there is no special benefit to adopting social norms, it is best to avoid social norms and adopt market norms.*

Final Thoughts

Even though this study was based on responses from more than 1,600 people and supported by considerable other research in social psychology, we probably need more studies along these lines. While we argue that it is best for a firm to avoid using social norms when they cannot be sustained, we also realize that the reason companies adopt social norms without thinking about the consequences is that the immediate rewards can be high. However, given that reneging on social norms after adopting them affects consumer experience in profound ways, including loss of trust and loyalty, companies may want to rethink the perils of adopting social norms when doing so is not sustainable in the long run. The other alternative is, of course, to adopt social norms and stick with them, even when it is temporarily not cost-effective. In short, we don't argue against companies adopting social norms and enjoying the benefits of doing so. But there is always a price to pay.

Customer defection can (and does) occur, even when market norms are adopted and maintained. But what this study shows is that when market norms are adopted, the intention to defect is substantially lower than when social norms are adopted and then abandoned.

Social norms don't come with an obvious price tag, but the benefits are not without a cost in the long run. There is an unspecified cost: reciprocity. Reciprocity is the price a company should be prepared to pay when it adopts social norms. If a company is not willing to pay, or cannot afford, the price, it is in its interest not to adopt social norms. There is no "free lunch" for companies; nor is there any for their customers.

REFERENCES

Ariely, Don. 2008. *Predictably Irrational*. New York: Harper Collins.

Augustin, C., and J. Singh. 2005. "Curvilinear Effects of Consumer Loyalty Determinants in Relational Exchanges." *Journal of Marketing Research* 42: 96–108.

Burton, Dan. 2005. "Americans Must Trust Vaccines for Avian Flu Plan to Be a Success." *The Hill* (November 15): 18.

Cialdini, Robert. 2009. *Influence: Science and Practice*. 5th ed. Boston: Allyn and Bacon.

Doney, P.M., J.P. Cannon, and M. Mullen. 1998. "Understanding the Influence of National Culture on the Development of Trust." *Academy of Management Review* 23 (3): 601–20.

Geyskens, Inge, Jan-Benedict E.M. Steenkamp, and Nirmalya Kumar. 1998. "Generalizations About Trust in Marketing Channel Relationships Using Meta-analysis." *International Journal of Research in Marketing* 15 (July): 223–48.

Gneezy, Uri, and Aldo Rustichini. 2000. "A Fine is a Price." *Journal of Legal Studies* 29.

Grayson, K., D. Johnson, and D. Chen. 2008. "Is Firm Trust Essential in a Trusted Environment? How Trust in the Business Context Influences Customers." *Journal of Marketing Research* 45: 241–56.

Hulme, George. 2005. "Lack of Trust Hampering Online Direct Marketing." *B to B* (October 10): 4.

Jap, Sandy D., and Shankar Ganesan. 2000. "Control Mechanisms and the Relationship Lifecycle: Implications for Safeguarding Specific Investments and Developing Commitment." *Journal of Marketing Research* 37 (2): 227–24.

Maltz, Elliot, and Ajay K. Kohli. 1996. "Market Intelligence Dissemination Across Functional Boundaries." *Journal of Marketing Research* 33: 47–61.

Rindfleisch, Arin, and Christine Moorman. 2003. "Interfirm Cooperation and Customer Orientation." *Journal of Marketing Research* 40: 421–36.

Starkman, Dean. 2005. "An Advisor to Trust." *Washington Post,* 18 September, F01.

Chapter 3

BRAND TREACHERY: THE FAILURE OF MARKETERS TO KEEP A BRAND'S POSITIONING AND PROPOSITION UP-TO-DATE

Alan C. Middleton, PhD, Schulich School of Business, York University

A brand name is more than the label employed to differentiate among manufacturers of a product. It is a complex symbol that represents a variety of ideas and attributes. It tells the consumers many things, not only by the way it sounds (and its literal meaning if it has one) but more important, via the body of associations it has built up and acquired as a public object over time.

(B.B. Gardner and S.J. Levy 1955)

About Brands

Judging by the number of books and articles on brands and branding, we are all now experts on the subject. From the ideologically biased and inaccurate *No Logo* (Klein 2000) to the great insights of Sidney Levy (Rook 1999) and Stephen King (Lannon and Baskin 2007), there is certainly a wide range of viewpoints. However, judging by the actions of brand marketers, brand management is still an art (albeit supported by science) and therefore subject to error and disaster.

Although this chapter will review some of the findings about brands, it is by no means exhaustive. It focuses on one of the key issues, brand loyalty, and examines a simple proposition: Unless the brand owner is loyal in keeping the brand's appeals relevant, differentiated, contemporary, and of good value, how can one expect a target user/purchaser to be loyal in either attitude or behaviour? Failure by a brand owner to fully engage with its brand in keeping its appeal up-to-date should be seen as an act of brand treachery.

The dictionary defines treachery as:

1. violation of faith; betrayal of trust; treason

2. an act of perfidy, faithlessness, or treason. (Dictionary.com 2008)

Whereas in the world of nations and politics, treachery is often intentional, in the world of brands it often is not. The 17th century French writer François VI, duc de La Rochefoucauld, made the following observation, which applies perfectly to brand treachery:

Treachery is more often the effect of weakness than of a formed design.

This chapter will examine this weakness. It is an especially serious weakness, given that a brand is, after all, a promise.

> *A brand is a promise of a consistently delivered quality of benefits and value that achieves the highest level of satisfaction versus direct and indirect competitors.* (Middleton 1996)

And breaking a promise is something none of us should ever do.

The Brand Loyalty Issue

One of the most critical notions and measures in brand value and brand equity is how loyal customers are to a particular brand. Both an attitudinal and a behavioural concept, the idea is simple: The better that a brand delivers benefits and value to its target group relative to the competition, the higher customers will value it and buy it more regularly.

Measures include tracking studies, share of wallet studies, and dash-boards. Share of wallet, for those who are unfamiliar with the term, is an analysis of what proportion of an individual's spending is on your product — rather than simply on what share of the overall market is yours. It could be possible, for instance, to have a large market share but few loyal customers — that is, many customers who buy your product some-times, due perhaps to circumstantial factors such as availability or price, but none who buy your product exclusively — that is, none who are truly loyal to your brand. A dashboard measures a number of factors — much as a car's dashboard might give you information about both external and internal factors, such as the temperature outside the car, the speed you are travelling, and the amount of gas in the tank — in order to make possible a complex analysis of marketing inputs (e.g., advertising and public relations investments) and outcomes (e.g., customer attitudes as measured by surveys, sales results). All of the measures related to brand loyalty focus on what the customer thinks and does for the brand versus its composition.

The principles of how companies persuade customers to give this loyalty are straightforward to state but complex to manage. Involved is a deep understanding of the target group's needs and wants; the appropriate design and pricing of the product or service; making the product or serv-ice, and information about the product or service (including, in some cases, the opportunity to sample, or "test-drive," it), readily available to the target customer; sufficient and appropriate communication of the ex-istence of the product or service; benefits to ensure the target customer is fully aware and motivated to purchase the product regularly; and well-organized, knowledgeable, and motivated employees who make the serv-ice elements a pleasure. In other words, brands that earn customer loyalty have a continuously effective marketing mix that takes account of changes in the business, customer, and competitive environments.

Overall, this requires seven rules — the Magnificent Seven Rules of Brand Management:

1. Stay in touch with the changing world around the customer and how this impacts his or her life and brand decisions.

2. Be consistent in keeping the promise of the commercial performance and functional benefits sought by the target customer and ensure that the brand continues to improve its performance and value in delivering what it is supposed to deliver. Sometimes this requires not just a continuous improvement approach but a revisiting of the basic business model.

3. Be consistent in keeping the promise of the commercial image/brand, meaning the benefits sought by the target customer. Ensure that the brand continues to improve its emotional benefits and value in delivering a distinctive image, meaning, and connection with its target group.

4. Be consistent in delivering not only these commercial benefits but also community benefits. In the 21st century, brands need to build an appropriate reputation on social and environmental issues: How the brand reflects community values is becoming an important factor in brand choice.

5. Be consistent in developing a corporate culture/value system that motivates employees to respond effectively, and with integrity, to each other, to suppliers, and to customers.

6. Engage in appropriate and constant updating of the marketing mix so that the brand does not fall behind competitors or customer expectations.

7. Integrate these efforts so that all elements work together to deliver a vital brand promise.

Challenges to Achieving Brand Loyalty

Keeping the customer's loyalty is getting harder to accomplish due to increased competition and customer expectations. Increases in competition come from not only other manufacturer brands but also intermediaries, like retailers' private label programs, especially as these are increasingly looking like brands! Furthermore, competition is now more global: No longer is competition just coming from North America, Europe, Japan, and Korea; now it also comes from Brazil, China, India, Mexico, and other emergent areas.

Expectations increase as customers network to share best stories, practices, and deals. Great service and product delivery in one category increases expectations in others, and communication of these experiences is fast and widespread. However, just because the job of keeping customers loyal is getting harder, brand owners should not give up. In a competitive world, anything less than constant understanding of customer needs and updating of the brand positioning and proposition must be regarded as brand cowardice and merits the term "traitor."

Here, then, is the question: How many companies are not following the principles outlined earlier and consequently losing user/purchaser loyalty? Right now, the evidence is limited and contradictory.

While there is a lot of conjecture about brands losing loyalty, there is no hard evidence available on the subject. However, all around us we see and read examples of brand owners...

▶ failing to invest in the appropriate research to determine the changing world of customer needs and wants;

▶ reducing the quality of a product or service to save money, rather than rethinking how to improve the quality and deliver improved value;

▶ making frequent price increases with no improvement in brand-delivered benefit;

▶ demonstrating laziness in the search for improvements in all aspects of the marketing mix;

▶ having one message delivered in communication, yet contradictory signals from pricing (e.g., constant discounting) and channel strategies (e.g., lack of availability when and where the customer wants it);

▶ failing to stay up-to-date in the distribution and marketing communications channels used;

▶ and, the biggest complaint recently, delivering poor customer service.

There is an old saying in brand management: "Brands don't die; they are murdered." This is so true: The so-called reduction in customer loyalty is in fact a reduction in brand-owner loyalty. For whatever reason, from "short term-ism" and false concepts of profit maximization to poor internal coordination systems and sheer laziness or stupidity, these brand traitors often kill, or substantially weaken, their customer-brand relationships.

Brand Loyalty Research in Canada

This notion of keeping a brand's positioning and proposition up-to-date is at the heart of the findings of research recently conducted by Leger Marketing. A survey of 1,502 adults across Canada in June 2008 revealed that while consumers viewed themselves to be fairly loyal to their brands, a major reason for those less loyal was that by failing to improve the brand's positioning and proposition, companies had allowed their product to slip until other brands had become pretty well the same — so there was no extra advantage in staying loyal to just one.

Loyal customers

First, the good news: Asked whether they were more or less loyal to consumer brands than they were three years earlier, most (65%) said that it was about the same for them. Further good news was that 15% said they were more loyal. The results are shown in Table 3.1.

_____ Table 3.1 _____

BRAND LOYALTY SURVEY,
PERCENTAGE OF CUSTOMERS WHO ARE LOYAL

Thinking about the main brands that you buy from supermarkets, drugstores, electronics stores or general merchandise stores, would you say you are, in general, more or less loyal to them than you were three years ago?

MUCH LESS LOYAL	SOMEWHAT LESS LOYAL	ABOUT THE SAME	SOMEWHAT MORE LOYAL	MUCH MORE LOYAL	DK/ NO ANSWER
4%	13%	65%	11%	4%	4%

Note: N = 1,502

Now, whether or not these perceptions are reflected in consumers' buying behaviour is a subject for further research, the point is that 80% of consumers in this survey saw themselves as being as loyal, or more loyal, than three years earlier. Why do they maintain loyalty?

The answers in the research are very clear. (See Table 3.2.)

_____ Table 3.2 _____
BRAND LOYALTY SURVEY, REASONS FOR LOYALTY

WHY DO CUSTOMERS MAINTAIN LOYALTY?	ABOUT THE SAME (N = 994)	SOMEWHAT OR MUCH MORE LOYAL (N = 201)
Brands continue to be appropriate for me and my lifestyle	56%	64%
My brands seem to have better value	40%	52%
My brands' quality has improved more than others	26%	41%
My brands come from reputable companies	30%	40%
My brands are more available than others	24%	30%

A couple of things are worth noting in this data: First, there are a substantial majority who believe that they are loyal to their brands and a number who have found reasons in an improvement in the marketing mix to become more loyal. This is good news for marketers. It demonstrates that, provided marketers follow the basics described earlier, there remains a propensity for consumers to continue to brand shop and remain loyal. Second, it shows that, in addition to the performance aspect of the brands and the benefits that they provide consumers (fit target group needs, value, quality, and distribution availability), the reputation of the company owning the brand is an important consideration.

This finding confirms other research globally. This is echoed in the conclusion of my recently co-authored book *Ikonica: A Field Guide to Canada's Brandscape* (Hanna and Middleton 2008). In this examination of successful Canadian brands, such as Tim Hortons, Canadian Tire, Cirque de

Soleil, Umbra, and WestJet, we conclude that three elements have come together to create these brands as icons in Canada: commercial benefits, cultural affinity, and community appeal, or "the three C's":

1. **Commercial benefits:** the value of the brand to its user/purchaser; what benefits it provides in performance and in image value versus the competition. In other words, what level of quality and trust does the brand deliver?

2. **Cultural affinity:** the fit of the internal culture of the organization that owns the brand with the wishes and desires for its attitude and behaviour by its user/purchaser group. Where does the company/brand stand on ethical, social, and environmental issues important to society, the community, and the individual buyer/user?

3. **Community appeal:** the fit of the brand with the social attitudes and behaviour of its targeted user/purchaser group. Does it reflect contemporary and "best behaviour" community values?

Increasingly, successful brand owners gain loyalty through not only the commercial proposition but also the shared values it demonstrates internally and externally on key social issues, such as ethical treatment of employees, suppliers, and the community; sustainable activities; and a demonstrated concern for the environment. Reputation risk is one of the important emergent areas for strategic discussion with major brand marketers.

Not so loyal customers

Let's move or to the less loyal.

Some 17% of the sample indicated that they were less loyal to their main brands than they were three years earlier: 13% said they were somewhat less loyal and 4% said much less.

The major reasons respondents saw themselves as much less loyal are outlined in Table 3.3:

_____ Table 3.3 _____

BRAND LOYALTY SURVEY, REASONS FOR DISLOYALTY

WHY ARE CUSTOMERS DISLOYAL?	MUCH/SOMEWHAT LESS LOYAL THAN 3 YEARS AGO (N = 273)
Other brands and mine are now all about the same quality	50%
Other brands and mine are equally available	48%
Other brands and mine are all equally appropriate for me and my lifestyle	43%
My brands seem to provide less value than others	34%
Other brands and mine all have about the same amount and quality of advertising and promotion	34%
Other brands and mine seem to offer about the same value	26%
Other brands and mine seem to come from equally reputable companies	18%

Other reasons for lower loyalty are mostly to do with perceived declines in brand performance. (See Table 3.4.)

_____ Table 3.4 _____

BRAND LOYALTY SURVEY, OTHER REASONS FOR DISLOYALTY

WHY ARE CUSTOMERS DISLOYAL?	MUCH/SOMEWHAT LESS LOYAL THAN 3 YEARS AGO (N = 273)
My brands are now less available than others	20%
My brands seem to have less or poorer advertising and promotion activity than others	20%
My brands' quality has not improved as much as others	19%
My brands no longer seem to be appropriate for me and my lifestyle	15%

The key theme here is not so much about an absolute decline in quality or value but a lack of ability to distinguish between their brands and others. As Peter Drucker once said:

> *If you're not different or better, you have to be cheaper.*
>
> (Drucker 2001)

Responses like those above indicate that owner disloyalty to their brands is not so much due to intent but, rather neglect, albeit often benign, on the part of the company. Unless a brand's positioning and proposition are kept updated and relevant, the brand either falls behind the competition or, equally as bad, is undifferentiated from its competition.

Cases in Brand Management — the Good, the Bad, and the Ugly

Let's look at some examples of brands that illustrate these findings.

The good

One example is President's Choice, a brand that was at the top of the list of Canadians' favourites in Leger Marketing's research. Why has this premium private label brand been so successful?

In my research on private labels, one respondent described it perfectly:

> *They (Loblaws) always capture the mood of the market, which I find really interesting... I think President's Choice has my number and that of most of my friends, to be really, really honest. I mean, I am their core client. I'm somebody who has a little bit of disposable income and can think about having fun so likes to try different things from different places.*
>
> – married working woman, early 40s, Toronto

In other words, in addition to some inherent advantages that come from being a retailer brand (display access, positioning opportunities versus manufacturer brands, and so on), Loblaws has constantly innovated and updated its products and brands: There is always news, new unique products, upgrading of quality, and innovation associated with the President's Choice brand.

Over 1,200 brands found in supermarkets, drugstores, electronics stores, or general merchandise stores were mentioned by the sample in Leger Marketing's research — we had asked the respondents to name up to five that they regarded as their favourites as a measure of attitudinal loyalty. (See Table 3.5.)

Table 3.5
BRAND LOYALTY SURVEY, MOST POPULAR BRANDS

OVER 10% OF SAMPLE MENTIONING	5-9% MENTIONING	3-4% MENTIONING	
President's Choice	Heinz	Dove	Toyota
Kraft	Tide	Coca-Cola	Crest
	Sony	Apple	Gillette
	Kellogg's	Pepsi-Cola	No Name
	Campbell's	Colgate	Nestlé

The broad range of familiar, well-established brands mentioned indicates the value of incumbency and also points to the resiliency of brands, which we will discuss later in this chapter.

For a second example of "the good," we will step outside of this list and examine Canada's favourite food place, Tim Hortons. Again, like President's Choice and other successful brands, it does the basics wonderfully well in the creation of a virtuous circle: convenient locations; good coffee and light food; clean, friendly surroundings; regular, friendly staff; good community connections; and a good place to go.

But, it does more; it regularly and frequently introduces new products. While this is no doubt a strain on the delivery system, this constant stream of new products means constant news (largely overcoming the need for discounting, like its competition) and the maintenance of the freshness of appeal of the Tim Hortons brand.

> We've gradually changed the fences of where the consumer lets us play. If we had tried to do a breakfast sandwich fifteen years ago, it would have been an absolute failure. Who would have thought that we could sell yogurt? We're constantly riding those fences. We listen to the consumer but we aren't prisoners to them. The current customer may not want this, but do we have enough of those current customers to keep the business alive long term? We haven't moved dramatically; we've just gradually moved the fences.
>
> – Paul House, Chairman, Tim Hortons
> quoted in *Ikonica* (Hanna and Middleton 2008)

Third, let's look at Canada's premier entertainment brand Cirque du Soleil. The story of this Quebec-based but worldwide phenomenon is the stuff of legend. Coming out of its founder's background as a street performer and the experience of street parties, Cirque has a strong value system that is focused around some fundamental aspects of innovation and integrity and a recognition that great brands are an unending story. Cirque's own value statements capture this:

▶ Creative driven: the very essence.

▶ Human-centric: inspired by life and emotions.

▶ Polymorphic, open architecture: open, diverse approach; patrons make their own stories.

▶ Introspective; evokes emotions: escape into imagination and dreams.

▶ Nomadic spirit: inspired by nomadic origins; of every culture and every country.

▶ Handcrafted: not mass produced; being one of a kind.

▶ Sensory abundance: colours, costumes, music, and intensity; strong sensory experiences.

In this way, Cirque manages its differentiation from Disney or Broadway. There is a clear "Cirque-ness" that anchors the brand as it moves from live shows to TV to several different productions. Cirque has an email subscriber/member list of over 2 million that keeps it connected to its loyal customers and uses other marketing communications as well. While this brand's storytelling could go stale, it hasn't yet!

There are many others I could mention: Canadian Tire, RIM's ubiquitous BlackBerry, WestJet, and a couple of the banks — notably Scotiabank and TD Canada Trust. Of course, there were other favourite brands that respondents mentioned in the Leger Marketing study that have followed the code of conduct to constantly update their commercial, cultural, and community appeals: Unilever's Dove is a recent standout example, Procter & Gamble's Tide is a long-running example, and Toyota, Apple, and Campbell's brands are all great examples of the restless and relentless updating of a brand's positioning and proposition that needs to be done by the brand owner. These are all brand "heroes" that stay loyal to providing the brand user/buyer with an ongoing reason to be loyal.

The bad

I define "bad" as those brands that are still "alive" and could be revitalized but are clearly breaking the code of conduct outlined earlier: that is, giving constant attention to, and updating, all of the three C's. These are the brand traitors that need to update their commercial appeals and/or pay more attention to the cultural and community aspects of their brands' appeal.

This view is supported by a 2006 survey conducted by The Strategic Counsel, *Canadian Business* magazine, and Cundari SFP. Called the "worst managed Canadian brands," their list (and mine) included the following:

▷ **Air Canada:** Whatever the turnaround in the recent past, and whatever sympathy one may have for it in an era of rapid fuel inflation, this organization's customer hostility shows in every move. It was by far the number one choice for worst managed brand in the 2006 survey, and there is no reason to believe that it would be any different today. Whatever the improvement in aircraft equipment and on-time arrivals, Air Canada still demonstrates:

- The "death by a thousand cuts" pricing approach: charging for absolutely every activity. This has made it the butt of comedians' jokes. ("They will be charging for the use of the oxygen masks next!")
- Overbooking and the bumping of even Elite customers.
- Poor in-flight, check-in, and reservation customer service.

As such, whatever attempts Air Canada has made to improve operations, many of which have been successful, the basic problem is a failure of customer-service orientation and, with that attitude, an inability to build a brand that Canadians have affection for and, with that affection, customer loyalty.

▷ **The "telcos":** Three out of the top 10 brands on the worst managed list were the three major telecommunications organizations: Bell/Bell Mobility and Express Vu led the group as the worst, but Rogers and Telus were not far behind. The issues for all of them lie in all aspects of the three C's but mostly in their pricing policies, or, should I say, the perceived lack of value delivered. Fortunately for their brand reputations, and for us as consumers, VOIP and newly authorized competition by the CRTC may force them to become more user/purchaser-friendly.

▷ **The energy companies:** The last group on the worst managed list were some of the energy companies. Specifically mentioned in the survey were Petro-Canada and Hydro-Québec, though I doubt that, on probing, the energy suppliers in other provinces of Canada would score much better. Again, this is an industry that has not demonstrated attention to the updating of its commercial proposition and has not integrated any meaningful activity in its cultural and community activity either.

The ugly

I define "ugly" as those brands that did not follow the principles outlined earlier and "died" because of it. I do not include those brands that disappeared because they were acquired — a very Canadian phenomenon that would require a different book to explain — but those that went out of business due to neglect and mismanagement. The standout example is Eaton's, about to be followed by North America's oldest brand, Hudson's Bay.

Eaton's is a Canadian tragedy. The department store concept started in France then moved to the UK, but in 1869 smart old Timothy Eaton brought the concept to Canada with its innovations to the traditional way of selling goods:

▶ a wide range of consumer goods in one location

▶ fixed prices rather than haggling

▶ a "goods satisfactory or money refunded" guarantee

▶ the Eaton's catalogue (1884)

▶ the move to shopping mall locations in the 1950s

The innovation in Eaton's approach was constant until the 1960s/1970s. Then the business landscape changed, with increasing affluence and the impact of the baby boom: New retailers emerged with new styles, experiences, and value offerings. The Eaton family kept pushing their management and staff back to the old department store model, confused cost cutting with strategy, and eventually murdered the brand.

A golden rule of branding is evident in the late 20th century history of Eaton's: Sometimes just a continuous improvement ("kaizen") approach to the commercial aspects of the brand is not sufficient. It all comes back to a reinforcement of rule #1 of the Magnificient Seven Rules: Stay in touch with the changing world around the customer and how this impacts his or her life and brand decisions.

Themes in Brand Successes and Failures

In his two books *Brand Royalty* (2006) and *Brand Failures* (2005), Matt Haig discusses some of the things that have succeeded and failed in brand management. It is worthwhile summarizing these, since they correlate closely with the key themes in this chapter.

In reviewing the survival of top brands, Haig emphasizes that owners must understand the core competencies on which their brands are built. He talks about 17 foundations for brand success, provided that the owners are "faithful to the cause" and loyal to the user/purchaser:

▷ **Innovation brands:** brands that have achieved their positions through innovation in either brand function or brand meaning. He cites Adidas, American Express, L'Oréal, Mercedes, and Sony as examples.

▷ **Pioneer brands:** brands that have pioneered new benefits or values: first movers. He cites Colgate toothpaste, Gillette, Goodyear, and Wrigley.

▷ **Distraction brands:** brands with a "fantasy" element that helps distract us from routine activities. He cites Barbie, Disney, and MTV.

▷ **Streamlined brands:** brands that retain a specific focus rather than broaden their appeal. He cites *Cosmopolitan* magazine, Toys"R"Us, and Subway as examples.

▷ **Muscle brands:** brands where size gives an advantage. IBM, McDonald's, Microsoft, and Walmart are some examples.

▷ **Distinction brands:** brands that have positioned themselves against an established brand with distinctiveness: Evian, Danone, Heineken, and Pepsi.

▷ **Status brands:** brands that signify wealth and status. Burberry, Moët & Chandon, and Rolex are mentioned.

▷ **People brands:** people as brands: David Beckham, Michael Jordan, and Oprah Winfrey are obvious examples.

▷ **Responsibility brands:** brands that need to convey corporate responsibility. Johnson & Johnson and M · A · C are great examples.

▷ **Broad brands:** broad in range and positioned in quality: Virgin and Yamaha, for example.

▷ **Emotion brands:** brands with which customers develop a strong emotional connection; these are brands that develop the most iconic status: Apple, Harley-Davidson, and Jack Daniel's.

▷ **Design brands:** brands based on powerful design insight: Bang & Olufsen, Vespa, and IKEA.

▷ **Consistent brands:** reliability and delivery on a consistent promise: Campbell's, Coca-Cola, and Nivea.

▷ **Advertiser brands:** brands where the symbolism of the advertising approach is key: Absolut Vodka, Calvin Klein, Gap.

▷ **Distribution brands:** brands whose core is convenient availability: Avon, Amazon, and Domino's Pizza.

▷ **Speed brands:** fast convenience in life: CNN, FedEx, Google, Reuters.

▷ **Evolution brands:** brands that help customers evolve or that are themselves moving up the value chain: HSBC, Intel, Samsung.

It goes without saying that when Haig goes on to describe brand failures, moving the positioning from its core proposition is one of the many failures in company loyalty to the brand that is evidenced. Others mentioned include:

▷ **Brand amnesia:** when a brand forgets what it is supposed to stand for (an extension of the brand foundation concept covered above).

▷ **Brand ego:** when a brand thinks that it can stretch to many segments, even if it is looking for slightly different sets of benefits.

▷ **Brand megalomania:** an extreme version of brand ego that the banks seem to be pursuing in the financial services market.

▷ **Brand deception:** while hyperbole done with humour may be acceptable, exaggerated claims set false expectations. When these are not met, brand credibility crashes.

▷ **Brand fatigue:** lack of creativity and innovation in all aspects of the brand's appeal.

▷ **Brand paranoia:** shown by a lack of focus or clarity in its actions: an over-reactiveness rather than proactivity in strategy and action.

▷ **Brand irrelevance:** missing the changes in the market (as described earlier with the Eaton's case).

These examples from Haig's books indicate certain critical success factors that we described earlier as the Magnificent Seven Rules of Brand Management.

However, the question should be posed: Does lack of attention and action mean certain death? No! One of the reasons there is so much interest in brands recently, and why getting the brand management right is so important, is that strong brands are amazingly resilient. Globally, several major brands were at the point of death and then revived themselves. In the next section, we will look at who they are and what they did.

Brand Revivals

In the last decade, some of the most famous and valuable global brands could have died but came back from the brink. Great brands have great resiliency; those that use this characteristic, along with the ability to change and innovate, can effectively relaunch themselves.

The Interbrand 2008 Most Valuable Global Brands listed the following top 12:

#1 Coca-Cola	$66.7 billion
#2 IBM	$59.0 billion
#3 Microsoft	$59.0 billion
#4 GE	$53.1 billion
#5 Nokia	$35.9 billion
#6 Toyota	$34.1 billion
#7 Intel	$31.3 billion
#8 McDonald's	$31.1 billion
#9 Disney	$29.3 billion
#10 Google	$25.6 billion
#11 Mercedes	$25.6 billion
#12 HP	$23.5 billion

At least six of these have had their troubles. Let's look at four of them in more detail: Coca-Cola, IBM, McDonald's, and Mercedes.

Coca-Cola

Throughout the 1970s, 1980s, and into the 1990s, during the cola wars of the time, Coke brand and the Coca-Cola company were fixated on the soft drink market and, specifically, on beating Pepsi. They got out of touch with their target market, let their understanding of the consumer wane, suffered the disastrous "new Coke" fiasco in 1985, and failed to introduce any new beverage products. They were in trouble. Then, a number of things happened: The global head of marketing, Sergio Zyman, hired a cultural anthropologist (a Canadian named Grant McCracken) to get them back in touch with their target group and started a revised approach to their marketing communications. Then, following Pepsi's example in noting the success of non-soft-drink beverages, they started on a program of new product development and acquisition — and, additionally, allowed their local subsidiaries more freedom to support brands with local market appeal. In the last decade, while things have not all gone smoothly, the Coke brand has revived and the company has a much broader offering of beverages. The Coca-Cola company is again growing at over 5% per year and has over 450 different brands worldwide, including waters, energy drinks, juices, coffees, teas, and, of course, soft drinks.

Lessons learned? First, a need to reconnect with the consumer target group's values, attitudes, and behaviour at more than a superficial level. Second, the need to rethink the business model. The assumption that a soft drink, even Coca-Cola, could ever regain its dominant position in the total non-alcoholic beverage market just did not fit the consumer realities of the late 20th and early 21st centuries. Coca-Cola had to reimagine the Coke brand as just one of — albeit a critical one of — a portfolio of offerings in the non-alcoholic beverage market.

IBM

Until Lou Gerstner took over IBM in 1993, the company business was primarily in the computer hardware market. While it had some software and outsourcing activities, its primary activity was in hardware and, despite the PC, what was known as the "big iron" (its mainframe computer). IBM's brand was powerful but declining. In fact, it was beginning to be a negative with some target groups: The Apple generation was beginning to believe that IBM stood for all that was out-of-date in computing. However, under Gerstner and his successor, Samuel J. Palmisano, who has been running the company since 2003, IBM transformed its business and its brand. Now primarily a services (55% of revenue) and software (20% of revenue) company, the brand has regained all of its former glory.

Lessons learned? Again, this is a reinforcement of the two principles mentioned earlier: Stay close to the changes in the business environment (the economy, demographic, and social trends, political and regulatory trends, technology and the competition) that affect your customer. Additionally, be prepared to make changes in your business model. IBM is still one of the most valuable brands in the world, but in the early 1990s it didn't look that way at all.

McDonald's

As recently as five years ago, McDonald's in North America had flat sales, seemed to be missing the trend towards healthier foods, and, despite continued growth internationally, was a "don't buy" recommendation from most analysts. Since then, boy, what a turnaround! Under its new, more contemporary advertising approach, "I'm loving it," introduced in 2003, McDonald's has introduced new menu selections and totally revamped its brand. It took a top-to-bottom approach — product, pricing, new areas for expansion, and new marketing communications — but, building on the strengths of the brand, North America is back to around 5% growth, and the analysts are in "buy" mode.

Lessons learned? Great brands have great resilience. In the words of my former colleague Marlene Hore, who at the time was national creative director at J. Walter Thompson, "Strong brands give permission to succeed and permission to fail...provided their owners find the answer to the contemporary wants and needs of the consumer in a reasonable time."

Mercedes

The brand is now so strong that the tendency is to think that it was always so. However, when Toyota launched Lexus in 1989, Mercedes gained the reputation of being an over-engineered, over-priced car for the elderly, and its sales and brand reputation suffered. Lexus established itself as a superbly engineered, high-value luxury car for the contemporary customer. As a result, Mercedes suffered — but then recovered. While Lexus has continued to thrive, Mercedes has more than recovered both its business and its brand reputation. Its main models were re-engineered, and new models were introduced, including some quite controversial ones, like the Smart car. New marketing communications initiatives were introduced, and a confirmed positioning as a luxury car for the youthful customer looking for that special Mercedes performance was successfully established.

Lessons learned? There is an ever-present need to keep a close eye on the competition. While the Mercedes brand and business did recover, it took time. Daimler had developed arrogance about its brand and position and ignored and underestimated the threat of the Japanese car makers. Keeping an eye on the competition means gathering enough information to *anticipate* competitive moves and decide what changes should be made in one's own strategy, not just responding after competitive action has been taken.

Lessons Learned: How to Avoid Consumer and Shareholder Groups Putting You on Trial for Brand Treachery

So what have we learned, aside from the obvious fact that brands are extremely valuable assets and need to be managed with the utmost care and professionalism?

At the heart of the issue is this: Brands that continue to provide a differentiated benefit, value, and satisfaction compared to their competitors develop more loyal, less price-sensitive customers — and this has value on not only the balance sheet as an asset but also the income statement as added profitability in comparison with weaker brands.

So, here are the 15 lessons learned; a restatement and an elaboration of the Magnificent Seven Rules of Brand Management mentioned earlier have been incorporated:

1. Stay in touch with the changing world around the customer (the economy, demographic and social trends, political and regulatory trends, technology, and competition) and how this impacts his or her life and brand decisions.

2. Be consistent in keeping the promise of the commercial performance functional benefits sought by the target customer, and ensure that the brand continues to improve its performance and value in delivering what it is supposed to deliver.

3. Be vigilant as to whether the basic business model behind the brand still has relevance. Sometimes commercial functional performance requires not just a continuous improvement approach but a revisiting of the basic business model.

4. Be consistent in keeping the promise of the commercial image/brand meaning benefits sought by the target customer. Ensure that the brand continues to improve its emotional benefits and value in delivering a distinctive image, meaning, and connection with its target group.

5. Be consistent in delivering not only these commercial benefits but also community benefits. In the 21st century, brands need to build an appropriate reputation on social and environmental issues: that is, how the brand reflects community values.

6. Be consistent in developing a corporate culture/value system that motivates employees to respond effectively and with integrity to each other, to suppliers, and to customers.

7. Be clear on the basic brand platform and core value. Let this guide areas for investment and improvement.

8. Engage in appropriate and constant updating of the marketing mix so that the brand does not fall behind competitors or customer expectations.

9. Integrate these efforts so that all elements work together to deliver a vital brand promise.

10. Great brands have resilience. This will give you time to fix errors and to catch up with competitive moves and consumer changes. However, those errors and deficiencies must be addressed: Resilience does not last forever.

11. Use both formal and informal research methods to describe and analyze the business environment, competitive strategy, and actions and their effect on your target customers. Don't guess. But also don't expect research to provide the answers — that's your job.

12. Make your research measures continuous so that you are constantly tracking on a dashboard or through a balanced scorecard,[2] the journey of the brand, and its story.

13. Try not to go head to head with current and potential competitors. Anticipate their moves. Be ahead of them.

14. Don't put juniors on this task. Brand management requires the energy of youth but also the wisdom of experience. It is a senior-level task.

15. Don't just do one-year plans. Brand management requires a longer-term perspective. At minimum, think in three- to five-year plans so that important changes can be put in place. But, equally, always look for immediate feedback that can provide the opportunity for improvement.

Fifteen lessons learned; all need attention. Adherence to only one or two will not a successful brand make. Attention to all 15 will enable you to be a brand hero, not a brand traitor. Don't be a brand traitor; your brand is worth fighting for!

> *A product is something that is made in a factory; a brand is something that is bought by a customer. A product can be copied by a competitor; a brand is unique. A product can be quickly outdated; a successful brand is timeless.*
>
> — Stephen King

REFERENCES AND BIBLIOGRAPHY

De Chernatony, L. 2006. *From Brand Vision to Brand Evaluation.* Oxford, UK: Butterworth-Heinemann.

Dictionary.com. 2008. "Treachery," from *Random House Dictionary*, at http://dictionary.reference.com/browse/treachery (accessed September 2008).

Drucker, Peter. 2001. *The Essential Drucker.* New York: Harper Business.

Ettenson, R., and J. Knowles. 2008. "Don't Confuse Reputation with Brand." *MIT Sloan Management Review* 49 (2) (winter).

Franzen, G., and M. Bouwman. 2001. *The Mental World of Brands.* Henley on Thames, UK: World Advertising Research Centre.

Gardner, B.B., and S.J. Levy. 1955. "Symbols for Sale." *Harvard Business Review* (March/April): 33–39.

Haig, Matt. 2006. *Brand Royalty: How the World's Top 100 Brands Thrive and Survive.* London, UK, and Sterling, VA: Kogan Page.

Haig, Matt. 2005. *Brand Failures: The Truth about the 100 Biggest Branding Mistakes of All Time.* London, UK, and Sterling, VA: Kogan Page.

Hanna, Jeannette, and Alan C. Middleton. 2008. *Ikonica: A Field Guide to Canada's Brandscape.* Vancouver/Toronto/Berkeley: Douglas & McIntyre.

Holt, D.B. 2004. *How Brands Become Icons.* Boston: Harvard Business School Press.

Interbrand.com. 2008. *2008 Best Global Brands Study.* Annual online report at www.interbrand.com/best_global_brands.aspx (accessed 5 May 2009).

Klein, Naomi. 2000. *No Logo: Taking Aim at the Brand Bullies.* Toronto: Knopf.

Knowles, J. 2008. "Varying Perspectives on Brand Equity." *Marketing Management* 17 (4) (July/August).

La Rochefoucauld, François (de), duc. 1930 (1665–1678). *Moral Maxims and Reflections.* New York: F.A. Stokes.

Lannon, J., and M. Baskin, eds. 2007. *A Master Class in Brand Planning: The Timeless Works of Stephen King.* Chichester, UK: John Wiley & Sons.

Scholz, Dave. 2005. "Brand Evaluation in Canada" in Research Report #14027-010 (Leger Marketing, 2008).

McCracken, G. 2005. *Culture and Consumption II.* Bloomington: Indiana University Press.

Middleton, Alan C. 1996. "Private Label or Public Brand: Branding Meaning Contrasts Between Retailer Brands and Manufacturer Brands of Grocery Packaged Goods." PhD diss., Schulich School of Business, York University.

Rook, D.W. 1999. *Brands, Consumers, Symbols & Research: Sidney J. Levy on Marketing.* Thousand Oaks, CA: Sage Publications.

Zyman, S. 2000. *Building Brandwidth.* New York: HarperCollins.

Chapter 4

HURTING THOSE WE SHOULD LOVE THE MOST

Douglas Olsen, PhD, Arizona State University

It is often noted that it takes much more work to acquire a new customer than to maintain an existing one. For this reason alone, one might expect that a company should focus extensively on issues of keeping existing customers satisfied — or at least not making them frustrated. Nonetheless, sometimes quite the opposite occurs: Perhaps in an attempt to bolster sales figures and increase market share, a considerable number of advertisements and promotions offer substantial benefits for new customers without making the same promotion available to people who already purchase the product or service. On such occasions, those who have been faithful to the company are, in essence, abandoned and watch with envy as strangers are welcomed with open arms.

Examples abound: A credit card company offers new clients a substantially reduced interest rate for six months if the balance from an existing card is transferred to them. Similarly, a bank may offer a product, such as a toaster, to those opening new accounts. Existing customers, some who may have been dealing with the bank for decades, have to sit by and watch as individuals with less than an hour of history with the bank take home the spoils. On one occasion, I asked my bank if I could have a free gift too, in this case an iPod, and explained that I had been a customer for 15 years. I was told very politely and sincerely that this was possible. The customer service agent patiently explained that what I would have to do was shut my current account down, take my money to another bank, and then come back, open up a new account, and transfer the money over. She was serious.

Fitness clubs tend to be notorious for this as well. In a quest to acquire new customers, they seem to have promotions that shift by the day. There used to be a fitness facility near my house, and I was constantly entertained by its efforts to grab customers: At one point in time, there was a sign advertising a new mountain bike with each yearly membership. The next time I drove by, it was offering to waive the initial registration fee. After this, the sign said something about a greatly reduced monthly fee, and the time after that, words proclaimed that there would be no fees at all for three months. I kept waiting for the offer where it would get someone to do the exercise for me — but that special never arrived on its promotion *du jour*. One can only feel sorry for the poor soul who signed up at some point in time, paid the standard registration fee, and agreed to the regular monthly instalment for a year. One can feel even sorrier for this person's friends, who probably have to regularly endure his tirades about how much better everyone else is treated.

Sometimes, advertisements will be self-comparative in nature. These take the general form of "Look at how much better we are now." A company comparing a new product to one of its own has a number of advantages: First, one would expect that perceived credibility should be high — who would know more about the improvements than the company itself? Second, relative to competitive comparison (e.g., "We are twice as good as our competitors"), self-comparative ads are less likely to evoke a strong counterreaction from competitors, either in the form of advertising or litigation. One possible downside, however, is that people who bought the previous model will be directly informed that the product they now own is inferior. One large motor-vehicle company introduced the 2007 model by comparing it to the 2006 version. Next to the 2006 version was "Vrooom." Next to the 2007 model was the extended word "Vroooooooom." Or, to paraphrase, if you purchased the 2006 version, that is too bad because it sucks.

In all of these cases – the credit card company, the bank, the fitness facility, and the automobile manufacturer – the intent was unquestionably never to harm existing and loyal customers. Yet the zeal to attract strangers may very well have sent negative signals and created hard feelings on the part of the customers who, arguably, should have been loved the most.

This chapter will review the findings from a survey that asked consumers specific questions regarding feelings of betrayal. The results are rather revealing and suggest that feelings of betrayal or being treated in an inferior manner are not uncommon. They also suggest that consumers are somewhat cynical about the motives underlying the behaviour of companies. After examining the research findings, a number of remedies are proposed for mitigating feelings of betrayal and dissatisfaction. These include: a consideration of the entire customer experience; keeping trust high; making existing customers feel special; and maintaining communication with the customer after the purchase has occurred.

Consumer Perceptions

Companies seek to build loyalty — a devoted adherence on the part of the customer, even in the face of reasonably attractive propositions by competitors. Indeed, many are deeply committed to tracking this dedication, monitoring churn (i.e., the turnover of customers), and other signals of loyalty. Even among those companies that do not formally track satisfaction, one would be hard-pressed to find one that suggests that it is not interested in building and maintaining a strong and loyal customer base. Given that customer loyalty is so highly coveted, one of the interesting ironies is that, on occasion, some companies are actually perceived to be disloyal to their own customers.

Organizational Hypocrisy — Betrayal of Customer Trust

On occasion, hypocrisy is present. A company wants the customer to be loyal to it; however, it takes actions that signal that it does not wish to be loyal to the customer. Situations where customers feel that they have intentionally and ruthlessly been taken advantage of are likely in the minority. But there are, of course, more subtle ways to betray the loyalty of those who have devoted their wallets to the company.

For example, such betrayal might transpire due to a customer service experience where there appears to be no desire to adequately resolve a problem; a promotional event in which the customer is not included; a breach of trust; or a violation of perceived equity (i.e., a person perceives that he or she has not got back what he or she put in).

Figure 4.1 presents results for the question "Have you ever felt betrayed by a company you were loyal to?" Note that it does not ask whether they have ever felt dissatisfied, miffed, or bothered but specifically whether they have ever felt *betrayed* (i.e., I was loyal to them but they were not loyal to me). Over one-third (36%) of the respondents perceived this to be the case. Only 50% could unequivocally respond that they have not.

While one could suggest that 36% of respondents does not constitute a majority, this number is substantial when one considers that in almost none of these cases was there likely an open desire on the part of the company to make the individual angry. Indeed, it would be interesting to go back to these companies and see if they even knew how, when, or where they had created this feeling. It is likely the case that most would not even know that such extreme feelings existed.

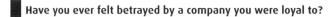

Figure 4.1

CUSTOMER FEELINGS OF BETRAYAL

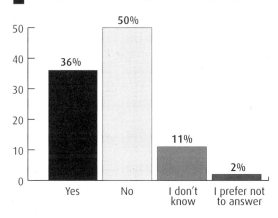

Note: N = 1,502

Treating New Customers Better Than Existing Customers

Work germane to this issue (Olsen, Lynch, and Argo 2007) indicates that consumers may experience a great deal of betrayal and anger in situations where a company offers a better promotion to new customers than they had initially received. It would appear that these individuals feel cheated and experience regret that they had not waited until later to purchase. Hence the response to the question "Have you ever felt that a company you were loyal to was treating new customers better than they were treating you?" is interesting. (See Figure 4.2.) A total of 45% of the sample indicated that they felt that this was the case.

Can you imagine how it would feel if your spouse was treating strangers with greater respect than he or she was treating you or that your kids preferred to hang out with the strangers down the street? The results from the survey suggest that almost half of respondents have felt this way in the marketplace. Again, it is likely not the case that this stems from wilful neglect but rather benign negligence.

_____ Figure 4.2 _____

FEELINGS THAT NEW CUSTOMERS WERE TREATED BETTER

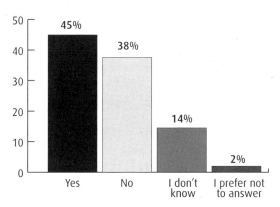

Have you ever felt that a company you were loyal to was treating new customers better than they were treating you?

Note: N = 1,502

People or Profits First?

Perhaps in order to compensate for a number of corporate ethics debacles in recent years, companies these days seem prone to adopt such slogans as "Put people first!" or "The customer is number one." Such slogans seem to imply that organizations are out to provide the highest of treatment for their customers, perhaps even at the peril of diminished profits. In the previous survey question, however, it was found that many people seem to think that companies treat strangers better than they treat their current customers. Beliefs such as this no doubt result in a more cynical, less-trusting customer. It is therefore interesting to examine a more general perception that the organization is *not* out to maximize the welfare of the customer.

In response to "What percentage of companies do you think care more about their profits than they do about their customers?" an average of 80% was observed. (See Figure 4.3.) While customers might not begrudge the organization for wanting to make a profit, companies should not labour under the assumption that their customers believe that they would do anything for them. While making profit and meeting the needs of customers may jointly occur, as evidenced by the results in Figure 4.3, 70% of respondents believe that a majority of businesses would put the pursuit of profit first.

_____ Figure 4.3 _____

BELIEF THAT COMPANIES CARE MORE ABOUT PROFITS THAN CUSTOMERS

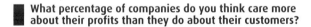

What percentage of companies do you think care more about their profits than they do about their customers?

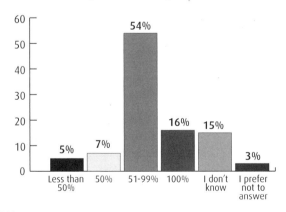

Note: N = 1,502

Are Special Offers for First-Time Buyers Effective?

Respondents were also asked "Have you ever switched to a company that was providing a special offer to first-time purchasers?" As presented in Figure 4.4, 55% indicated that they had switched under these conditions. This is instructive on a number of fronts. First, the tactic of running such specials does appear to be effective at migrating many customers over — hence businesses are reinforced for such actions. Second, for many companies, perceptions of customer loyalty may overinflate the number of people who are truly dedicated (i.e., there are probably many people who would be willing to switch if given the right incentive).

These results also likely demonstrate myopic thinking on the part of the customer. Let us suppose that you see someone cheat on his or her partner and then he or she come up to you and tell you how much he or she would like to be with you. Given the previous behaviour, would you be a little wary? Might you not believe that this person will do the same thing to you later on? However, we know that consumers typically make decisions based on short-term considerations. They will happily take the company up on this "first-time purchaser" offer but, in essence, reserve the right to complain in the future about how the company does not treat its existing customers as well as strangers. Customers can be fickle.

_____ Figure 4.4 _____

EFFECTIVENESS OF SPECIAL OFFERS FOR FIRST-TIME PURCHASERS

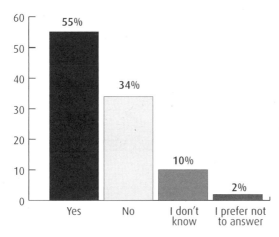

■ **Have you ever switched to a company that was providing a special offer to first-time purchasers?**

Note: N = 1,502

Implications for Business Practice — Avoiding Perceived Betrayal

These results indicate that businesses should be concerned about how their actions may be resulting in a perception of betrayal among their loyal customers. In general, most customers are cynical regarding the operating motives of organizations, perceiving them to put profits ahead of people. One area where this may be problematic is when businesses are perceived to be engaged in profit-seeking behaviours that treat new customers better than loyal patrons (i.e., betraying the ones the company should love the most). It is argued that this betrayal rarely stems from an overt desire to rebuff a customer; rather, it is based on myopic vision and a focus on short-term goals only. A number of remedies are proposed to counter these tendencies and consequently reduce the amount of perceived betrayal: (1) consider the entire customer experience, (2) keep trust high, (3) demonstrate loyalty to existing customers, and (4) engage in ongoing communication in order to gauge (dis)satisfaction. Each of these is examined in turn.

Consider the entire customer experience

More and more recognition is being given to managing the entire customer experience. This practice suggests that greater efforts must be given to understanding what the customer encounters regarding the organization *prior* to acquisition (e.g., word of mouth, advertising), throughout the acquisition (e.g., working with the salesperson), during use, at the point of disposal, and then, perhaps, during reacquisition. While most companies are willing to give assent to this notion, the problem is that, frequently, companies are fragmented, with different groups working with very different incentives. For example, the salespeople are geared towards customer attainment, and the customer service people are focused on customer retention. Chances are, each group is trained and rewarded accordingly. Hence, in many ways you cannot blame a salesperson for aggressively pursuing new customers by offering incentives to get them in the door — even if it is at the expense of existing customers.

Salespeople are not thinking long-term, and they are not really focused on existing customers; they are concentrating on the "new." Given their druthers, they would probably not want to upset or offend current clientele, but their focus for the day is on generating more revenue.

Moving beyond the front-line personnel, there are many other areas of the company that may benefit from a customer-centric perspective. Accounting and finance will have to get on board if resources are going to be dedicated to ensuring a positive customer experience from start to finish. Management will have to recognize that a pushe in sales promotion to boost revenue for a given quarter might be good, but other resources and programs may be needed to ensure long-term customer satisfaction. Indeed, myopic programs that pull people in the door only to inadvertently disappoint, annoy, or betray them a short while later do not seem like a good strategic plan.

Keep trust high

Sometimes we forget how important trust is in a capitalistic society and how many of our actions are contingent on it being in place. Those who have had experiences dealing with Eastern Europe or China during periods when capitalistic systems were not yet developed to North American standards can attest to the differences in mentality that existed. More specifically, it would seem that in early stages of capitalistic behaviour, the focus is almost exclusively about short-term profit realization and not on trust, much to the peril of long-term relationships. While profit is still of importance in a North American context, there is usually at least a tacit understanding that a long-term existence is forged through behaviours that foster trust-based relationships. When trust is present, variations in product and service delivery are more likely to be attributed to external causes than malicious intent. Both critical transaction points and elements of trust formation are important in determining the level of trust that might be present.

Critical Transaction Points There are a number of areas where transactions may go awry and perceptions of risk can be great. These are points where trust may be gained or lost. While the specific nature and importance of each may vary depending on the industry, three key risk elements are present: (1) product/service class risk, (2) product/service specific risk, and (3) transaction risk.

First, there is risk associated with the product/service class. In general, the acquisition of medical procedures, investing in the stock market, or speculating in real estate may be perceived to be more risky than shopping for groceries. Where such variance is perceived to be present, additional work is needed on the part of management to underscore what is done differently by the organization to reduce risks below industry standards.

Second, there may be a perception of risk associated with the product or service itself, independent of the industry. A person might see the computer industry as risky but a particular product as quite safe, or vice versa. Will the product do for me what I want it to do for me? Will it work the way it should? Here, relational trust may be buttressed with formal mechanisms (e.g., warranties or third-party endorsements) and a focus on effective communication (i.e., ensuring that individuals have an accurate understanding of the product, what it does, and how it does it).

Third, transaction risk can be a major concern for some individuals. While this is definitely true when purchasing online, it can be equally true in face-to-face transactions. If a given product or service was ordered, will what I asked for actually be provided? Will the information provided be kept safe from computer hackers and therefore safe from identity theft? Will customer details be shared with other parties for the purposes of marketing?

Elements of relational trust There are a number of key characteristics of relationships that must be addressed for trust to be present and grow. Much of this stems from seminal research in the field of services marketing (Parasuraman, Zeithaml, and Berry 1985). The core constructs are:

▷ **Knowledge:** Does the company have a great deal of knowledge regarding its products and services?

▷ **Empathy:** Does there appear to be concern on the part of the company and its representatives for the well-being of the customer?

▷ **Responsiveness:** Is the problem handled quickly?

▷ **Reliability:** Is there consistency in the products and services that are offered (i.e., does the person get what they expect to get, time after time)?

▷ **Problem-solving orientation:** Does the company seem more interested in solving the problem or selling a product/service?

▷ **Honest and open communication:** Is there sufficient two-way dialogue between the customer and the company?

Linking this back to the concept of betrayal, while stellar performance on all dimensions may be difficult to achieve, most customers likely believe that the company will make stringent efforts to ensure a quality relationship. A significant breach on one or more of these dimensions may cause a strong disjuncture between the relationship that was expected/hoped for and that which actually occurred.

Demonstrating loyalty to existing customers: making them feel special

Most customers are likely savvy enough to recognize that a business has to engage in growth strategies and that part of this includes the acquisition of new customers. The positive treatment of one does not, however, need to mean the poor treatment of the other. Nonetheless, there should be a conscientious effort to ask "What are we doing to make sure that our existing customers' needs are being taken care of?" and "Is there anything we can do to proactively demonstrate that we care about them?"

One mechanism to make existing customers feel special would be to implement some form of loyalty program. Research has demonstrated that, if designed properly, these programs can be very effective at decreasing defections (increasing the customer lifetime), fostering additional purchases, increasing share of wallet,[3] and yielding insight into the buying behaviour of the member. The impact of the program may differ depending on the pre-existing loyalty. For individuals who display a lower level of patronage, these programs have been found to increase the amount and type of sales. However, for those who are already fairly dedicated customers, such programs are effective at maintaining spending and increasing the customer lifetime.

While such programs may spur increased loyalty, they have a potential downside if improperly executed. This speaks to the need to consider up-front what purposes the loyalty program will serve and what goals one seeks to meet. The best and brightest of these programs result in a more extensive relationship with the customer, not just cash savings. In line with this, they should generally be geared towards those who will purchase more, not just those looking to save a few dollars. Further, it is important to realize that there are different types of incentives that may be put in place to deal with different consumer motives: (1) economic rewards that foster monetary savings, (2) hedonistic rewards that provide gifts and luxuries, (3) social-relational awards that provide people with information about events and make them feel like they are part of a group, (4) informational advice that gives access to specialized material, and (5) functional rewards such as priority service (phone numbers, lineups, etc.) (Meyer-Waarden and Benavent 2008).

Ongoing communication to gauge (dis)satisfaction

We know two things about customers' post-purchase behaviour: (1) only a minority of dissatisfied customers will complain, and (2) if complaints are resolved promptly and positively, the net result may be a more loyal customer. Consequently, the key question from a marketing perspective is: What is being done to adequately understand where problems are occurring so that they can be addressed before they get out of control? On a passive level, there may be systems in place where customers can provide feedback (e.g., a 1-800 number, an email address, or a website where they can type in comments). The mere presence of such systems, however, is not necessarily sufficient. In order for them to be effective, a number of hurdles must be overcome.

First, is it clear to customers to whom they should email or talk in order to resolve any frustrations that they are having? Second, are customers actively encouraged to voice their opinions and share their concerns? Third, is this process perceived to be difficult or convoluted? Fourth, is there a perception that contacting the company will actually be a positive and problem-resolving experience? (That is, even if customers know whom to call, if they believe that this effort will be fruitless they are not likely to do it.) Until these questions are answered, the lack of complaints should not necessarily be considered a sign that all is well in customer land.

Beyond passive systems, companies may benefit from more structured research efforts. Focused efforts to understand specific elements of the customer experience can be of value. These might be of a one-off nature, conducted either by in-house personnel or by consultants studying a specific problem (e.g., performing an intensive analysis of a bottleneck in the order-fulfillment process). Alternatively, they may be of a more regular nature. One such survey might be administered to *all* customers following a purchase and/or a fixed time period later to determine what, if any, problems or areas of disappointment have emerged. Another type of survey might be some form of satisfaction tracking administered on a regular basis to a portion of customers in order to alert the organization to unanticipated downtrends (i.e., those which might prompt immediate and intensive investigation) or determine whether different types of customer-centric programs are having a positive impact.

While formal efforts, either passive or active, can be extremely valuable, informal mechanisms can be of benefit as well. Having salespeople or managers contact patrons after a sale to make sure everything is in satisfactory condition would make a strong statement regarding the concern the company has for the customer. It would: (1) bolster many, if not all, of the aspects involved in building relational trust, such as empathy, problem orientation, and open communication, and (2) help to identify where problems exist and what remedial actions might be needed to fix the issue. So why does this not occur more often? A number of possible reasons spring to mind. It is likely the case that many sales personnel are not rewarded for creating long-term satisfaction — once customers are out the door, their job is done. This is likely exacerbated by the fact that if they are on the phone, they are not making a sale and therefore falling behind in personal revenue and corporate sales quotas.

Another possible contributor is that there may be some degree of apprehension regarding what might be heard — human nature is such that most of us would likely prefer to live in a state of ignorant bliss than to actively seek out problems to fix. However, not finding out about a problem does not make it go away. For some customers, such problems may result in a great deal of frustration, perhaps to the point where they feel that what they expected from the company and what was delivered are poles apart. Such frustration, if not remedied or if dealt with in a callous fashion, may ultimately lead to a sense of betrayal.

Results presented in this chapter demonstrate that many customers feel that companies are more concerned about profits than they are about the interests of customers. Indeed, many have felt a sense of betrayal and/or that first-time customers receive better treatment than those who are loyal. It is hard to imagine that any company would wilfully promote such feelings. Rather, they are likely created out of short-term thinking that may result when trying to determine how to effectively acquire new customers. Acquiring new customers and maintaining loyalty to existing customers are not mutually exclusive. To this end, the following are suggested: (1) appropriate internal communication to ensure that individuals seeking to acquire new customers are working in lockstep with retention efforts, (2) developing appropriate loyalty programs, and (3) ensuring that mechanisms are in place to monitor and respond to customer complaints.

REFERENCES

Meyer-Waarden, Lars, and Christophe Benavent. 2008. "Rewards that Reward." *Wall Street Journal*, 22 September, R5.

Olsen, Douglas, Christopher Lynch, and Jennifer Argo. 2007. "The Negative Impact of Self Comparative Advertising." European Association for Consumer Research Conference, in July, in Milan, Italy.

Parasuraman, A., Valarie A. Zeithaml, and Leonard L. Berry. 1985. "A Conceptual Model of Service Quality and Its Implications for Future Research." *Journal of Marketing* 49: 41–50.

Chapter 5

MEASURING LOYALTY

Christian Bourque, Leger Marketing
Arancha Pedraz-Delhaes, Leger Marketing
Dimitra Maniatis, Leger Marketing

From both academic and managerial points of view, brand loyalty is a variable of strategic importance, since it both impacts brand equity and is linked to the firm's competitive advantage. Some consider brand loyalty the primary goal of marketing, and it is often identified as the ultimate dependent variable in marketing research models. As we will discuss here, while marketing companies have become very sophisticated in defining this ultimate dependent variable, consideration for the independent variables going into the model has not undergone any serious paradigm shift.

This chapter will discuss four topics: The first part is devoted to the evolution of the definition of brand loyalty when it comes to capturing the different dimensions that compose this complex concept; the second and third parts look at how academics and the market research industry have tried to identify the drivers of loyalty and how, collectively, our research may not have succeeded in actually finding what makes loyal customers tick; and, finally, the fourth part gives a broader perspective on the customer experience, the ultimate objective being to measure how brands are disloyal to customers and how this may affect their future behaviour.

Brand Loyalty 101

The concept of brand loyalty has generated considerable interest among academic researchers since the early 1950s, when serious research on consumer behaviour became popular, and has received extensive exposure since then. The numerous approaches used by researchers have led to a large range of definitions. Despite some obvious contradictions, a historic overview reveals a certain evolution and some general trends.

The earliest studies on loyalty concentrated on its behavioural outcome, defining the concept as the consistent repurchase of the same brand over time and using brand choice sequences such as sequence-of-purchase (Brown 1952), proportion-of-purchase (Cunningham 1956), and probability-of-purchase (inspired by Markov chains). The 1950s and 1960s brought the development of many repurchase predictive models. However, their effectiveness is questionable and this approach failed to understand the properties underlying brand loyalty. Indeed, as we now know, the predictive power of behavioural models is fairly low. All of us can think of certain products we buy and re-buy, yet we know that we could switch brands tomorrow without blinking. For example, one can be loyal to a car insurance company for years and then switch, without a second's consideration, for a reduced rate. Why? Because that customer was loyal only in his or her behaviour yet had not developed any emotional relationship with the brand.

The inclusion of an attitudinal dimension to brand loyalty, which appeared in the 1960s and became more dominant in the 1970s, allows for a better understanding of the phenomenon. For example, Day (1969) introduced the notion of brand preference in the definition of brand loyalty. Loyalty was not a simple question of repurchase behaviour any more: A truly loyal customer must be consistent in both behaviour *and* attitude. An important difference was established between "intentional" loyalty and "spurious" loyalty (e.g., the repurchasing of a brand for reasons of availability or price). Some researchers began to concentrate almost exclusively on the attitudinal component of brand loyalty, insisting on the psychological attachment or commitment to the brand and completely abandoning the behavioural outcome of brand loyalty.

Nowadays, brand loyalty tends to be considered as a multidimensional construct. Authors generally define brand loyalty as a repeat purchasing behaviour based on cognitive, affective, motivational, or conative[4] factors (e.g., Macintosh & Lockshin 1997; Oliver 1999).

The Drivers of Brand Loyalty: Measuring Tomorrow Today

The extensive literature summarized above has tried to define the concept of brand loyalty — in other words, the current level of loyalty of a given customer. However, beyond the measurement of present brand loyalty, academics and managers are even more interested in predicting future brand loyalty. In other words, what can we measure today that will allow us to infer that future actions on the brand will yield predictable results? The identification of brand loyalty antecedents has been, and continues to be, a very prevalent topic in the scientific literature. Unfortunately, findings are contradictory and somewhat inconclusive.

In spite of this, researchers often link the variable of satisfaction to loyalty (e.g., Howard & Sheth 1969; Engel & Blackwell 1982; Taylor & Baker 1994). Indeed, it is very easy to assume that satisfied customers will be loyal to the firm and, conversely, that loyal customers are probably satisfied. With this mindset, many authors have worked on determining the elements of a company's offer (e.g., the factors that impact a product or a service's perceived quality) or image (i.e., corporate reputation) and customer characteristics (e.g., expectations, attitudes toward the brand, brand convictions) that impact on customer satisfaction and, ultimately, loyalty. Yet the causal relation between satisfaction and loyalty has been taken for granted and very rarely examined in detail.

And, surprisingly, when tested, a moderate to low correlation coefficient was found between the two constructs (Bloemer & de Ruyter 1998; Johnson et al. 2001; Mittal & Kamakura 2001; Szymanski & Henard 2001). Some authors (e.g., Duffer & Moulins 1989) stated that satisfaction can explain loyalty intentions but is not always an accurate predictor of the effective buying behaviour. In other words, the survey might measure that the customer intends to be loyal because he or she is satisfied but does a poor job of measuring his or her actual future behaviour. Moreover, research proved that the direct effect of satisfaction on loyalty varies between different products and different industries. At best, research has shown that satisfaction is a necessary condition for loyalty but is certainly not a sufficient condition in explaining the essence of the concept. The challenge, then, lies in identifying all the other factors. Why does satisfaction not systematically translate into customer loyalty? Why do satisfied customers leave? Why do dissatisfied customers not necessarily switch brands or service providers?

The market structure is one possible explanation. Brand differentiation, the absence of competitive brands, or the lack of accessibility of these alternatives (the financial cost of change, for example) can artificially create loyalty. Most often, we remain loyal out of habit or out of lack of capacity of the competition to attract us. Therefore, some researchers have suggested thinking of loyalty in terms of customer commitment. Questions like "If you could turn back time, would you still choose brand/supplier ABC?" were proposed to measure this concept. The "too many good reasons"[5] question of the Conversion Model™ (one of the world's leading brand commitment research models) was designed to address this same issue.

Intention to recommend has also been presented as a good indicator of customer commitment or loyalty. Reichheld (2006) argued that the likelihood to recommend question was the most effective way to measure loyalty and predict short-term purchase. The author developed the "net promoter score" by subtracting "detractors" (customers showing the lowest likelihood to recommend) from "promoters" (customers giving high likelihood to recommend scores). This score can then be calculated for each company, which allows benchmarking by industry. This new way of looking at loyalty, using likelihood to recommend, introduces the notion of risk for the customer: "Can he or she take the risk of recommending a brand to a friend?" Commitment to a brand must be strong if people are willing to transfer part of the brand's promise onto their own shoulders. What if they are wrong? What happens if the brother, mother-in-law, or colleague does not like the brand? In one simple question, "The Ultimate Question" (Reichheld 2006), we were getting closer to the true nature of brand loyalty. This approach is both economical and simple and allows for direct measurement. Although this new approach has aroused a lot of enthusiasm, it still needs to be used with caution, since independent studies found little predictive value to the net promoter score (Morgan & Rego 2006; Keiningham et al. 2007).

Indicators or predictors of loyalty remain a controversial issue in marketing research, with consultants promoting different "magical" measures and academic researchers being unable to reach a consensus with their contradictory findings. Since brand loyalty is a complex construct with various underlying dimensions, and given the existence of many possible moderating variables, perhaps loyalty measurement requires a broader approach. If neither satisfaction nor likelihood to recommend is sufficient to measure loyalty, perhaps, if both concepts are correlated to the ultimate variable, it could be useful to combine these two indicators.

For instance, the Leger Marketing Canadian Disloyalty Index takes into account customer satisfaction and likelihood to recommend, but to fully triangulate the concept of disloyalty we added a third indicator: likelihood to switch to another supplier. Why this third measure? Countless examples exist of customers who, while they may not be truly satisfied with their supplier, may not like it enough to recommend it either but remain loyal because they do not want to move. Adding this component to loyalty helps refine the construct by focusing on potential behavioural outcomes. The total score, based on the three measures, becomes an informative performance measurement for each individual company, while the overall sector-based data collected allows for industry rankings and benchmarking. The Canadian Disloyalty Index at the end of the chapter shows the scores by industry and for the main players in each sector.

Once Measured, What Impacts Loyalty?
The Traditional Company-centric Approach

Marketers and the market research industry have struggled with the concept of brand loyalty for 40 years now. However, in the quest for the holy grail of an explanation of loyalty, it may not be the construct of loyalty that is, in fact, the key issue. Rather, the issue may be the perspective from which we have sought to measure that construct. The problem is identifying ALL the key drivers of loyalty in a company's product or service offering and leaving out the variables that only have a spurious relationship with loyalty.

Traditionally, companies have had a tendency to compartmentalize loyalty. The general pattern was that companies would use the very broad notion of loyalty as the outcome (the dependent variable) but study only a very small portion of the explanatory variables (the independent variables) that may cause disloyalty or loyalty. Very often, the champion of the satisfaction tracker and the champion of the brand tracker were two distinct persons in a given company, both focused on loyalty but through very different prisms. One was focused on what part of the product offer best explains why customers are satisfied, while the other was focused on what part of the brand promise (tangible and intangible) gives customers that "feel good" element that the company would tell its advertising agency to build on. This disjointed approach would lead the first agent to adopt a very operational perspective on loyalty (improve attribute X or Y of the product), while the second agent would provide a more "aerial" perspective on the brand's positioning.

As the two silos move across time, both are preconditioned to see loyalty as being the natural outcome of something the company does or an element that is purposely part of the brand's proposition. In other words, the inputs into each loyalty model, whether it is satisfaction-oriented or branding-oriented, will be based on the product or service characteristics the company wishes to put forward. With this mindset, researchers will find that some scores are statistically significant (since so many variables are correlated), while others are not, and recommendations will be made as to what needs to be changed in the product or service offer to increase a loyalty score.

This traditional approach to brand loyalty has several flaws: The first flaw is the lack of a single integrated tool that measures customer experience as being a composite of one's tangible (usage and satisfaction) and intangible experience with the brand (how the customer feels when using this brand or how he or she feels about using this brand). Once these are integrated, the challenge would be to find, between industries, the relative importance of usage and satisfaction versus the emotional commitment to a brand. However, using both dimensions within the same instrument may shed light on the respective role of each dimension. A more holistic approach to customer experience may be needed.

The second flaw concerns the fact that the attributes that are part of the model are determined by the actual characteristics of the product or service and identified by those who work (too) closely with the brand. This acts just like putting blinders on the research. The results of the research will inevitably lead to a biased outcome, suggesting that moving one or several indicators up will increase the ultimate indicator (loyalty). Brands will therefore make changes to the variables they wish to, or can, control within a closed system of attributes they have designed but that the customer did not choose.

Consider the example of a grocery store chain: This chain's main positioning is offering the widest variety at a lower price. In their brand tracker, managers will seek to obtain customers' ratings on such things as freshness, quality, price, variety, proximity, and availability of private brands. These are the attributes they want to champion and believe matter most to customers. Let's say a customer has visited this chain a couple of times. In the brand tracker, this customer gives 8, 9, or 10 out of 10 on all the indicators about which the store cares but grades very low on loyalty. The model would interpret that as a fluke, an illogical respondent who likes us but is committed somewhere else, etc. However, this customer has an entirely different interpretation: He or she does not want to go back because the chain forces shoppers to bag their groceries themselves. But this variable is not part of the model. Would it make sense to ask "On a scale from 1 to 10, how satisfied are you with bagging your groceries?" No. But what if customers were asked at the store's exit: "Please tell us everything about your shopping experience that was not right." The opinions of this same customer would be richer and more meaningful.

What about another grocery store that does not allow customers to take their carts to their cars? The store claims that carts were stolen in the past or that some customers were not disciplined enough to leave them in the designated area. So the chain penalizes 99% of their loyal customers for 1% of abusers. What happens to the customer who needs to carry six bags of groceries and a tired one-year-old in his or her arms, in the rain, to his or her car at the other end of the parking lot? He or she would be right to never set foot in this grocery store again. However, would this silly rule likely be part of the grocer's brand tracker, its satisfaction monitor? Of course, the question is only rhetorical....

The idea is to get better knowledge of "tipping points" when a loyal customer (according to all dashboard[6] variables) becomes disloyal and to measure what the company has done wrong and whether customers will forgive it.

The third flaw lies in the fact that these models will often not consider variables that are very important to consumers because companies feel they cannot do much about them. If they are not important to the company's internal processes, therefore they must not be important to customers. Understanding the "power of inertia" (not wanting change, not wishing for something different, insecurity regarding alternatives, risk, etc.) is rarely a research objective. The same reasoning applies to understanding how customers feel about things that an industry sector does not do and how it influences the perception of a brand.

Consider one example: Canadian wireless providers do not allow customers to carry over unused minutes in their price plans. This is something the entire industry does not do. But the fact that one's own supplier does not allow it is, of course, of greater importance than the fact that the competitors do not allow it. It is a variable that directly influences loyalty and satisfaction but that is not measured by the industry — because the industry does not do that. The perverse effect of this is that no one in the industry knows what would be the return on investment of doing it. How would it lower churn? Would customers forgive a supplier for a few dropped calls if it offered the service? Could the price of monthly plans be increased in exchange? What would be the impact on market share?

A New Customer-centric Approach to Measuring Disloyalty

The fundamental problem with traditional approaches is that — and this book strongly disputes this paradigm — they consider the consumer as the loyal or disloyal entity. Therefore, the traditional approaches will usually fault the customer for leaving. Research results will be interpreted as evidence that the consumer is wrong in evaluating the relative performance of a brand or product, cannot truly understand a company's competitive advantage, or did not seek or get the right information. Haven't we all heard these board room conclusions? Much of this is due to the common use of only a subset of the actual tools that would help better understand the customer.

The science of understanding loyalty is somewhat like meteorology. We now have a powerful thermometer (our Canadian Disloyalty Index, for example), a powerful barometer, and all the other tools that exist to measure the weather, but predicting what next weekend will be like is still a challenge!

Some of the tools needed to better develop our brand loyalty strategy already exist but are not in common use. Yet they will need to be integrated into one's brand dashboard as regular measures. They are:

▷ **Dissatisfaction trackers:** Limit the research only to customers who are not fully satisfied, and only ask questions about why they are not fully satisfied rather than the traditional "How satisfied are you?"

▷ **Churn studies:** Talk to customers who have left you, and get direct input on the customer experience variables that led to them leaving (failure in customer service, competitor offers, etc.).

▷ **Measurement of irritants:** This would require companies to break down their customers' entire experience with the brand and seek to understand where along the way the company goes wrong, without focusing on what it does right. Questions would need to be worded to elicit insight into what could have been done better, what could be improved, what do competitors do at this same moment that we could do ourselves, etc. If possible, the same research could be conducted with the competitors' clients as well.

▷ **Risk assessment research:** In a world where budgets to improve customer experience are as inelastic as customers' price perceptions, risk assessment research may help pinpoint the areas of customer experience where not investing is *not* causing disloyalty, versus the areas where lower performance drives customers over the tipping point of having to waste time, energy, and resources to become disloyal.

The science of understanding customer satisfaction has greatly evolved. Now, more than ever, we better understand not only the value of loyalty research but also its limitations. The future of this industry can be even brighter if we decide to go over to the "dark side," which involves moving from a company-centric to a customer-centric approach to loyalty.

Instead of looking at ourselves in the mirror and liking what we see, through the traditional paradigm, approaches do exist for looking directly into our customers' eyes.

The Leger Marketing Canadian Disloyalty Index

The Leger Marketing Canadian Disloyalty Index started off as a task in understanding how satisfied Canadians were with the companies and industries that they interact with most often. In the process of developing this index, some key questions were raised about how satisfaction and loyalty are related and how they interact with each other. Here, we will review the process and the inputs that went into this index and discuss the results of a nationwide study that was conducted to understand satisfaction and loyalty. Or, in our case, disloyalty.

Customer satisfaction measurement is a performance measurement. It measures how an organization's product or service performs in relation to customers' requirements. It has been determined that:

▶ 1 dissatisfied client talks to 13 other clients.

▶ 1 satisfied client talks to 5 other clients.

▶ 96% of dissatisfied clients don't talk about it.

▶ 91% of dissatisfied clients don't come back.

▶ 95% of dissatisfied clients come back when the cause of their dissatisfaction has been rectified.

Satisfaction, commitment, and loyalty are driven by a number of dimensions, all of which need to be measured to gain a holistic understanding of the customer-brand relationship.

As has already been mentioned in this chapter, customer satisfaction and commitment/loyalty should not be measured independently. We need to understand the relationship between them and how they affect each other. As a result of our findings and dealing with some of the issues around satisfaction and loyalty when we started this process, we realized that many companies have "satisfied" customers, but many also have "disloyal" customers.

The Leger Marketing Canadian Disloyalty Index takes into consideration both satisfaction and loyalty. It comprises a set of questions we consider to be the most predictable and, more important, those it is most possible to take action on. These questions include the following:

▶ overall satisfaction

▶ likelihood to recommend

▶ likelihood to switch

▶ brand/supplier most likely to be switched to

To create the index, we completed a total of 2,100 online interviews, in both English and French, among a representative sample of Canadians across the country aged 18 years or older. In the Canadian Disloyalty Index, a company can score between 100 and 200 points, according to how the following three questions are answered:

▶ overall satisfaction

▶ likelihood to recommend

▶ likelihood to switch

In the following pages, we will look at specific industries and discuss those that have been able to create a loyal customer base and those that have created volatile relationships with their customers, thus resulting in a disloyal customer base. We will also discuss industries that have the appearance of loyal customer relationships but in fact rely on other factors to maintain their clients.

The figures provided for each industry — which plot loyalty on a four-quadrant graph showing passivity, loyalty, loyalty indifference, and disloyalty — take into account only the likelihood to recommend and likelihood to switch attributes. The size of the bubbles in the charts represents the number of survey participants rating that specific industry or company. The lines used in the figures represent the likelihood to recommend and likelihood to switch means (averages) for each industry and, in the case of the overall results, the means of all industries combined. When we add customer satisfaction into the disloyalty score, we come up with a list of the players in order from most disloyal customers to least disloyal customers. (See the tables provided.)

Overall Canadian Results

Looking at Figure 5.1, one can see that there are great differences in customer disloyalty in the 16 different industries represented. However, in addition to looking at each industry as it is rated, we need to keep in mind that there are some industries that are more heavily regulated than others, and consumers react differently to these industries depending on the economic conditions. In industries that are considered "free market," such as supermarkets, quick serve restaurants, mass merchandise stores, etc., consumers have choices, and their loyalty is dependent on many different

variables. In industries that are more regulated, or those that are oligopolistic (i.e., competition is limited to a small number of producers or sell-
ers), consumers understand that their choices are more limited, and loyalty
could be swayed by that fact alone.

_____ Figure 5.1 _____

MAPPING LOYALTY/DISLOYALTY FOR 16 INDUSTRIES

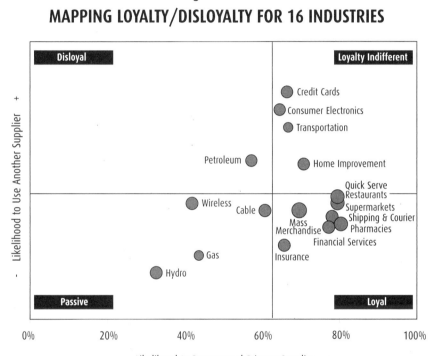

In industries such as petroleum and consumer electronics, price and convenience play a big role in customer disloyalty. For petroleum, we often
go to the gas station that is closest to our home or work, or to the one
that has the lowest price that day. And, if your car is running on empty,
it's probably rare that you will seek a particular gas station to fill up.
Whether gas costs $1.35/litre or $.65/litre, need drives purchase in this
situation. In consumer electronics, due to the high price of many items
and consistency of product selection, the supplier with the lowest cost

will get the business, and it becomes very difficult to build a loyal client base. The 54-inch "X" brand of television is the same whether it's purchased at Best Buy, Future Shop, or another retailer. The price on a higher-end item such as that, however, is a key differentiating factor when deciding where to purchase. To combat this issue, many petroleum and consumer electronics retailers have implemented client loyalty programs. Most petroleum companies have points programs in place, and suppliers in the electronics industry often offer price guarantees if you provide them with a flyer advertising a lower cost. Strategies like these have helped to create a more stable client base but not necessarily a loyal one.

The credit card and wireless industries are interesting cases because of the nuances within each of them. Credit cards are very easily interchangeable, since most consumers carry more than one. Often, credit cards also offer incentives to consumers (such as low interest balance transfers or point programs) to sway them. More and more, competitors in this industry are partnering with as many companies as they can to offer the incentives that their customers are looking for. Many have relationships with Aeroplan and Air Miles, and many are approaching retailers to offer retailer-specific cards with retailer-specific points. Maintaining loyal customers in this industry is very difficult. A good incentive program and the ability to continually offer more than the competition are key.

The wireless industry scored very high in disloyalty for various reasons: First, consumers don't like the fact that they are locked into long-term contracts, and they are often dissatisfied with the service from their wireless provider. Then, the wireless industry is notorious for offering their existing customers "device upgrades" at a low cost to ensure that they lock in those customers for another two- or three-year term. Those choosing not to enter into a long-term contract end up paying full price for their device, which could be hundreds of dollars more than the "upgrade price." They also offer new clients plans that have a three- or six-month "free" airtime option, while the customers that have been with them for a long time end up paying more and more for their mobile plan each time they renew their contract. Dissatisfied customers in this industry often change suppliers regardless of the cost to get out of their contracts, and this has been made easier with the recent number portability legislation. As was mentioned previously, it's easier (and often cheaper) to keep your current customers than to gain new ones. Why, then, is the wireless industry so keen to disappoint its current clientele?

In industries such as hydro, gas, and cable, by contrast, consumers often don't have a choice about which supplier to use, so, regardless of their satisfaction, they are not likely to switch. These customers aren't loyal; they just don't have the opportunity to be disloyal.

Home improvement and mass merchandise retailers have a challenge in maintaining loyal customers as well. In these industries, price and convenience play a big role in loyalty (or, again, in this case, disloyalty). When purchasing small/inexpensive items, convenience drives shopping behaviours. In instances where big-ticket items are being purchased, consumers are driven mostly by price. Customers are more likely to be loyal to a retailer such as Costco or Sam's Club because they have paid a membership fee. In the home improvement sector, both price and expertise of the staff play a big role, followed by convenience.

Quick serve restaurants — that is, QSRs — scored well in the disloyalty index. Much of that score can be attributed to coffee purchases. Most coffee drinkers are very loyal to their coffee retailers and will make their coffee purchase a routine (e.g., purchasing on the way to work or on their coffee breaks). In the fast food section of this industry, the "healthier alternatives," such as Subway, have managed to build a more loyal client base than others.

Financial institutions, pharmacies, and insurance companies have done a great job of developing a client base that is loyal. It can be argued that customer loyalty is highly impacted by the type of relationship that a client has with a company. For example, it's difficult to change financial institutions because there is an established relationship and, in many cases, a contract (e.g., a mortgage) that isn't easily moved from one financial institution to another. In the pharmacy category, people generally have a relationship with their pharmacists and develop a level of trust. The pharmacist also has a history of the medications that the customer has taken, or is taking, and can advise the customer about issues that are important to his or her health, such as side effects and drug interactions.

However, it is very important that these types of industries take care in ensuring their client base is satisfied. Even though it's more difficult to change suppliers in these sectors, an unsatisfied customer will find a way to switch. We often see clients of financial institutions switching suppliers when their mortgages expire. This can be a result of getting a better interest rate, but often it is because the client is dissatisfied and doesn't want to deal with his or her current financial institution any more.

_____ Table 5.1 _____

TOP (MOST DISLOYAL) SECTORS, CANADIAN DISLOYALTY INDEX

	DISLOYALTY RANKING	DISLOYALTY SCORE	CSAT SCORE*	LIKELIHOOD TO RECOMMEND SCORE	LIKELIHOOD TO SWITCH SCORE
Retail Electronics	1	103	70	65	6
Wireless Providers	2	103	56	43	−41
Credit Cards	3	98	78	69	16
Petroleum	4	96	71	56	−19
Home Improvement	5	94	71	72	−21
Transportation	6	94	70	69	−2
Cable Providers	7	89	66	60	−46
Mass Merchandise Retailers	8	82	75	71	−45
Gas	9	80	63	44	−67
Hydro	10	80	58	34	−76
Quick Serve Restaurants	11	75	89	80	−38
Shipping & Courier	12	73	82	78	−52
Supermarkets	13	72	85	80	−43
Insurance Companies	14	70	76	67	−64
Pharmacies	15	63	91	81	−57
Financial Services	16	62	80	77	−59

Note: A high disloyalty score indicates that a company's customers are less loyal (that is, more disloyal) than those of companies with a lower disloyalty score.

* CSAT = Customer Satisfaction

Retail Electronics Industry

Retail electronics is a very price-sensitive industry and, as can be seen in Figure 5.2, none of the major players has a loyal customer base. Future Shop has the most disloyal customers in this industry and ranks fifth for disloyalty from the nearly 100 companies that were tested. Source by Circuit City falls in the middle of the pack, and although Best Buy boasts the most loyal customers in this industry, the company still ranks in the top 20 companies for disloyalty overall.

_____ Figure 5.2 _____
LOYALTY/DISLOYALTY FOR THE RETAIL ELECTRONICS INDUSTRY

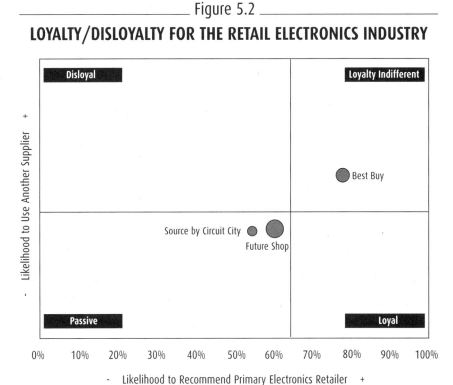

Before adjusting for overall satisfaction, consumers primarily shopping at Source by Circuit City and Future Shop appear to be passive, and those primarily shopping at Best Buy appear to be loyalty indifferent.

Once the score for customer satisfaction is accounted for, however, Best Buy customers prove to be the most loyal, with a disloyalty score below the industry average of 106.

Since price is the highest driver in this industry, retailers have started offering "lowest price" guarantees and will offer consumers electronics at a discounted price if they can bring in proof that another retailer has the same product for a lower price. Good service and knowledgeable staff are also key in this industry, since many consumers are not technologically savvy and require assistance when choosing various products. In addition, there are many smaller electronics retailers that we could not include in our study, so the competition for these three big players is by no means small. We can even find electronics available at mass merchandise stores and supermarkets, which makes the competition even stiffer. And, since customers are now using the Internet to do price comparisons more than they ever have in the past, retailers need to keep juggling all the loyalty drivers to ensure customers keep coming back. Balancing price, knowledgeable staff, and good customer service is critical for this industry.

_____ Table 5.2 _____

DISLOYALTY INDEX, RETAIL ELECTRONICS INDUSTRY

	DISLOYALTY RANKING	DISLOYALTY SCORE	CSAT SCORE	LIKELIHOOD TO RECOMMEND SCORE	LIKELIHOOD TO SWITCH SCORE
Future Shop	1	111	66	60	13
Source by Circuit City	2	107	71	55	14
Best Buy	3	93	73	78	-7

Wireless Industry

Due to the contractual nature of the wireless industry, customers are less likely to switch wireless providers, forcing a somewhat loyal customer base for companies in this industry.

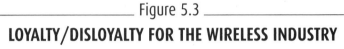

--- Figure 5.3 ---

LOYALTY/DISLOYALTY FOR THE WIRELESS INDUSTRY

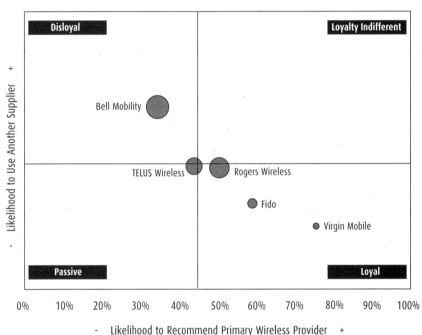

As seen in Figure 5.3 and Table 5.3, the companies that have the most disloyal clients are also the companies whose primary customers are most likely to switch providers. Bell Mobility has the most disloyal customers in this industry because its customers are not very satisfied, less likely to recommend them, and more likely to switch to another provider. Virgin Mobile, Fido, and Rogers have the most loyal clients, with disloyalty scores below the industry average of 104.

While customers who say they would be inclined to switch wireless providers generally don't know who they would switch to, Rogers and TELUS are the more common choices. With recent number portability legislation and foreseeable deregulation in this industry, these companies will have a hard time trying to justify their practices to their long-term customers. Why would a customer who has been with a given company for 15 years have to pay more for a mobile phone than a new customer? Why are these companies punishing the customers who have given them their business year after year?

I can't remember a time when my wireless provider called and said "You've been with us for 15 years. To show you we value your business, we would like to offer you a new phone that is not available on the market yet, free of charge." Wouldn't rewarding my 15-year loyalty with this company make me an advocate for them? Keeping customers "satisfied" when they reach out is just not enough any more. To build loyal customers, companies have to do things for their customers that are unexpected, that show customers how much they are valued.

Table 5.3

DISLOYALTY INDEX, WIRELESS INDUSTRY

	DISLOYALTY RANKING	DISLOYALTY SCORE	CSAT SCORE	LIKELIHOOD TO RECOMMEND SCORE	LIKELIHOOD TO SWITCH SCORE
Bell Mobility	1	114	52	33	−25
TELUS Wireless	2	104	55	43	−44
Rogers Wireless	3	99	58	50	−46
Fido	4	81	68	59	−60
Virgin Mobile	5	60	73	76	−66

Credit Card Industry

The credit card industry is one that has a very hard time maintaining loyal customers, since most of us carry more than one credit card and use them interchangeably. Often, consumers — especially those who are younger and those who are trying to establish a credit history — apply for the credit card offered by their financial institution, since the card that they are most likely to be approved for is with a financial institution with which they have some history. After a credit history is established, however, the incentives provided by each card start to play a much bigger role in the consumers' minds. Whether consumers prefer to get points towards merchandise, cash back, or air travel rewards, they can find many different cards that offer what they need.

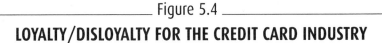

Figure 5.4
LOYALTY/DISLOYALTY FOR THE CREDIT CARD INDUSTRY

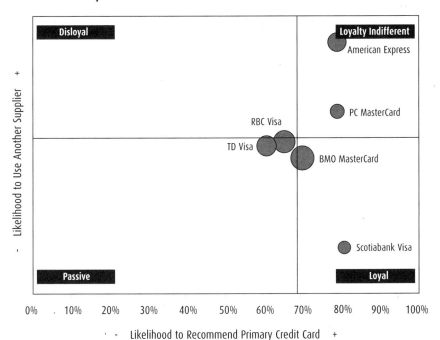

In this category, American Express has the most disloyal client base, probably due to the perception that it is not as widely accepted as other credit cards and is sometimes more difficult to get approved for. Canadians who primarily use their American Express cards are much more likely to use another credit card than those who primarily use a Visa or MasterCard. Those who primarily use their Scotiabank Visa, PC MasterCard, RBC Visa, or BMO MasterCard are the most loyal (below the industry disloyalty average of 98). They are satisfied with their credit card, likely to recommend it, and not too likely to use another credit card.

With most Canadians having two or three credit cards in their wallets, it is important for these companies to constantly keep on top of what types of rewards their customers are looking for. Many companies have done a great job looking at the various demographics that make up their card membership and tailoring products to suit each one of them. Although the credit card industry is still very price sensitive when it comes to interest rates, consumers also want to get something back for their loyalty.

_____ Table 5.4 _____

DISLOYALTY INDEX, CREDIT CARD INDUSTRY

	DISLOYALTY RANKING	DISLOYALTY SCORE	CSAT SCORE	LIKELIHOOD TO RECOMMEND SCORE	LIKELIHOOD TO SWITCH SCORE
American Express	1	110	74	79	−49
TD Visa	2	104	69	61	−14
BMO MasterCard	3	96	82	70	−8
RBC Visa	4	93	88	66	−16
PC MasterCard	5	93	84	79	−25
Scotiabank Visa	6	84	77	80	18

Petroleum Industry

While the petroleum industry is largely price- and convenience-driven, there are not a lot of players with which to compete, which provides some loyalty for companies within this industry. With most consumers purchasing gas at a station that is close to their homes or on their way to work, most have a routine or preferred supplier when given a choice. However, need drives this purchase and since the product is more or less identical from one supplier to the next, most customers will seek low price and, if necessary, go to another supplier to fill up.

_____ Figure 5.5 _____

LOYALTY/DISLOYALTY FOR THE PETROLEUM INDUSTRY

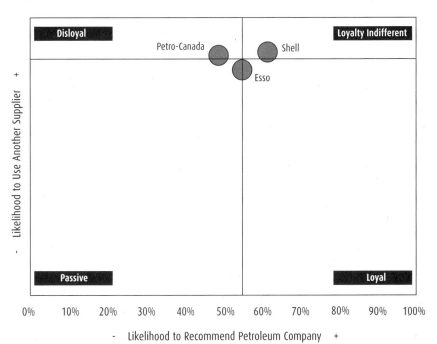

Looking at Figure 5.5 and Table 5.5, it appears as if Esso may have more loyal customers than Petro-Canada or Shell. However, when customer satisfaction is accounted for, Petro-Canada and Shell are below the industry average of 97 in terms of disloyalty, making Esso the company with the most disloyal customer base. And while most Canadians who are inclined to switch from their primary petroleum supplier are unsure about who they would switch to, Petro-Canada appears to be the most common choice.

Competitors in this industry have done a good job of trying to maintain a loyal client base, offering their customers points programs, co-branded credit cards, and other perks for staying loyal. Most have increased the amount of retail space to fulfill our constant need for one-stop shopping and tried to accommodate our increasingly time-driven lifestyles by providing coffee, snacks, and other sundries. But is it enough? Are we as loyal to our petroleum companies as we're ever going to get? Are they loyal to us? Probably not. Gas prices are exactly the same from one gas station to the next, and you have to wonder how that happens. These companies need to do a lot more to ensure we keep coming back. Sure, gas is a necessity, but there is always a gas station five minutes down the road that you can go to instead.

Table 5.5

DISLOYALTY INDEX, PETROLEUM INDUSTRY

	DISLOYALTY RANKING	DISLOYALTY SCORE	CSAT SCORE	LIKELIHOOD TO RECOMMEND SCORE	LIKELIHOOD TO SWITCH SCORE
Esso	1	103	66	48	−17
Shell	2	94	72	62	−15
Petro-Canada	3	93	74	55	−23

Home Improvement Retail Industry

In a knowledge-based and price-sensitive industry such as retail home improvement, overall satisfaction can make a difference in terms of customer loyalty.

_____ Figure 5.6 _____
LOYALTY/DISLOYALTY FOR
THE HOME IMPROVEMENT RETAIL INDUSTRY

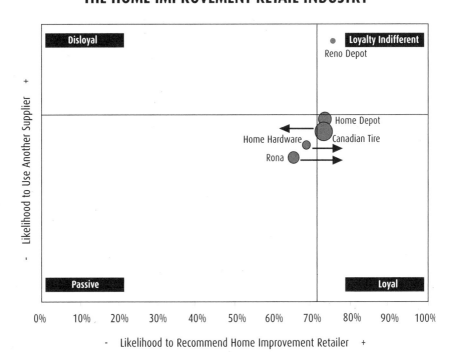

When looking at Figure 5.6, it appears as if Canadian Tire and Home Depot have the most loyal client base in this industry. However, when adjusting for customer satisfaction and the fact that primary customers of Home Hardware and Rona are less inclined to switch to another home improvement retailer, the latter two companies actually have the most loyal customers. The arrows indicate where these companies would be if customer satisfaction had been included.

Canadian Tire and Reno Depot are above the industry average of 95 for disloyalty. Offering a better customer experience, Home Hardware, Rona, and Home Depot are below the industry average for disloyalty and, with a more personalized shopping experience, Home Hardware actually boasts the *most* loyal customers. Canadians who are inclined to switch from their primary home improvement retailer to another most commonly say they would go to Home Depot, while Home Depot customers say they would choose Rona. Retail store location primarily drives this result.

So how did Home Hardware build such a loyal client base? Most of us recognize the recent "Homeowners helping homeowners" slogan. (Actually, the musical version is going through my mind as I'm writing it!) Home Hardware realized that it couldn't compete with Home Depot or Rona on price. Not to say that its prices are more expensive, but the organization's purchase power when it is dealing with its own suppliers is notably lower. Instead, Home Hardware took a more customer-centric approach, ensuring that the people who are helping its customers are knowledgeable and have the background to answer questions. People who are undertaking renovations appreciate this and will keep coming back for the knowledgeable and personalized service they receive.

_____ Table 5.6 _____

DISLOYALTY INDEX, HOME IMPROVEMENT RETAIL INDUSTRY

	DISLOYALTY RANKING	DISLOYALTY SCORE	CSAT SCORE	LIKELIHOOD TO RECOMMEND SCORE	LIKELIHOOD TO SWITCH SCORE
Reno Depot	1	99	75	76	12
Canadian Tire	2	96	71	73	−21
Home Depot	3	94	74	73	−15
Rona	4	93	73	65	−32
Home Hardware	5	84	65	68	−27

Transportation Industry

In the transportation industry, customer satisfaction and price drive consumers' decisions about their supplier of choice. With customer satisfaction playing such a huge role in this industry, transportation providers have the opportunity to develop and maintain a loyal client base. Unfortunately, once customers are disgruntled, it is especially difficult to sway their opinion of a provider. As this industry becomes more fee-based, price will become a bigger driver of disloyalty. The fees most providers now charge for checked baggage, in-flight refreshments, headphones, and other items are making consumers more price-conscious than they used to be.

_____ Figure 5.7 _____

LOYALTY/DISLOYALTY FOR THE TRANSPORTATION INDUSTRY

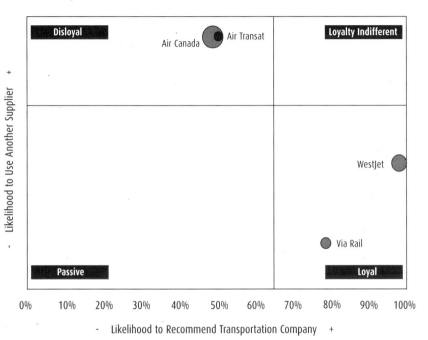

While WestJet and Via Rail both rank below the industry average of 98 for disloyalty, Air Canada and Air Transat, with their much lower customer satisfaction and likelihood to recommend scores and the fact that their primary customers are much more inclined to switch to another transportation provider, are well above the average in terms of disloyalty. And, as seen in Figure 5.7 and Table 5.7, WestJet and Via Rail have the most loyal client base. Their customers are highly satisfied, likely to recommend them, and not inclined to switch to another transportation provider.

Air travel has changed dramatically in the last 20 years and not necessarily for the better; that is why Air Transat and Air Canada find themselves as the top two companies for disloyalty. Gone are the days when these companies appreciated their customers and showed it. Now, in addition to all the "extra fees" we are enduring, their service is declining and so is their reliability. And although we acknowledge that these companies face some challenges as well (i.e., gas prices), they are not offering their customers anything to offset their inferior service offering.

––––––––––––––––––––––––––– Table 5.7 –––––––––––––––––––––––––––

DISLOYALTY INDEX, TRANSPORTATION INDUSTRY

	DISLOYALTY RANKING	DISLOYALTY SCORE	CSAT SCORE	LIKELIHOOD TO RECOMMEND SCORE	LIKELIHOOD TO SWITCH SCORE
Air Transat	1	126	63	50	32
Air Canada	2	125	52	49	31
Via Rail	3	63	81	79	–57
WestJet	4	55	91	98	–35

Cable/Internet/Satellite Industry

Looking at the cable, Internet, and satellite industry, it is evident that the companies who have the most loyal client base are those who service areas for which they are the only choice for consumers. With the regional footprint these companies have established, users have limited choice of suppliers, unless they go the satellite route.

_____ Figure 5.8 _____

LOYALTY/DISLOYALTY FOR THE CABLE/ INTERNET/SATELLITE INDUSTRY

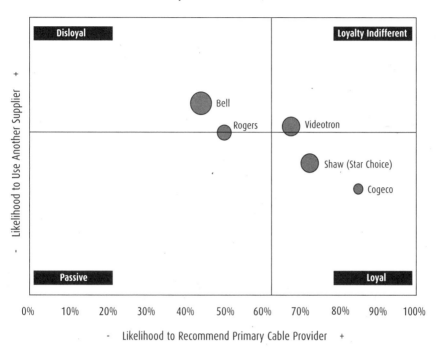

Rogers and Bell are above the industry average of 90 for disloyalty, rating lower in terms of customer satisfaction and likelihood to recommend and higher in terms of likelihood to switch, resulting in these companies having the most disloyal customers. As these competitors often operate in the same areas, competition is high between them; when asked which supplier they would switch to, Rogers customers indicated Bell and Bell customers indicated Rogers. Maintaining a satisfied and loyal customer base is especially important for these two competitors.

As shown in Figure 5.8 and Table 5.8, Cogeco and Shaw (Star Choice) are the companies with the most loyal client base. They rank below the industry average for disloyalty as their customers are not inclined to switch providers, are satisfied with their provider, and would recommend them.

More and more consumers are looking for alternatives to these service providers and, although the industry in Canada is still heavily regulated, there will come a time when consumers have more choices. How will these players compete in that market? Customers don't easily forget how they have been treated, and if these providers don't become more loyal to their customers, their rate of defection will increase significantly in the coming years.

_____ Table 5.8 _____

DISLOYALTY INDEX, CABLE/INTERNET/SATELLITE INDUSTRY

	DISLOYALTY RANKING	DISLOYALTY SCORE	CSAT SCORE	LIKELIHOOD TO RECOMMEND SCORE	LIKELIHOOD TO SWITCH SCORE
Bell	1	106	59	45	−33
Rogers	2	92	61	50	−45
Videotron	3	82	80	68	−43
Shaw (Star Choice)	4	77	68	73	−58
Cogeco	5	65	80	85	−69

Mass Merchandise Retailer Industry

The mass merchandise retail industry should probably be split into a couple of groupings. On the one hand, you have Costco, Price Club, Walmart, and Zellers, which often compete for the same customers, and, on the other, The Bay and Sears, who are in direct competition with each other. Customers who pay an annual membership fee to Costco or Price Club are obviously more loyal to this retailer than the more price-conscious customers of Zellers and Walmart. Although these retailers do have some loyal customers, price is a much bigger factor for their customers.

_____ Figure 5.9 _____

LOYALTY/DISLOYALTY FOR THE MASS MERCHANDISE RETAILER INDUSTRY

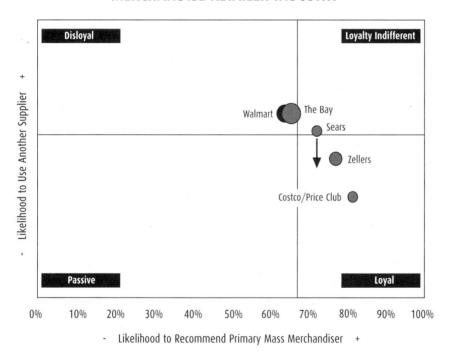

Considering the industry's average disloyalty score is 87, Walmart and The Bay are well above it, scoring 92 and 93 respectively. Sears, on the other hand, has more loyal clients than it appears in Figure 5.9. While Sears customers are more inclined to switch mass merchandisers than Costco/Price Club customers, higher customer satisfaction for Sears brings the company's loyalty second to Costco/Price Club. When asked which retailer they are most likely to switch to, Costco, Price Club, and Zellers customers said they would go to Walmart, while Walmart primary shoppers are most likely to switch to Zellers.

So, what has Costco done to ensure it has the most loyal client base in this industry? If you've ever been to your local Costco store on a Saturday or Sunday afternoon, you know that waiting in line to pay will take you longer than picking up all the things you need in the store. And, with Costco's exclusive arrangement with American Express, shoppers have limited payment options available to them. Some believe that these customers have a false sense of perceived value associated with shopping at this type of retailer. Others say it's because the retailer is membership-based, which gives consumers a sense of exclusivity. But, with the highest likelihood to recommend score and the lowest likelihood to switch score, Costco is obviously doing something right and making its customers feel valued.

_____ Table 5.9 _____

DISLOYALTY INDEX, MASS MERCHANDISE RETAILER INDUSTRY

	DISLOYALTY RANKING	DISLOYALTY SCORE	CSAT SCORE	LIKELIHOOD TO RECOMMEND SCORE	LIKELIHOOD TO SWITCH SCORE
The Bay	1	93	68	66	−36
Walmart	2	92	68	64	−36
Zellers	3	84	78	77	−49
Sears	4	70	84	73	−40
Costco/Price Club	5	66	81	82	−66

Residential Gas Industry

The next two industries we're going to look at are interesting because consumers' choice of providers is limited. This lack of choice makes consumers of residential gas and hydro very passive, placing these two industries right in the middle of our index.

_____ Figure 5.10 _____

LOYALTY/DISLOYALTY FOR THE RESIDENTIAL GAS INDUSTRY

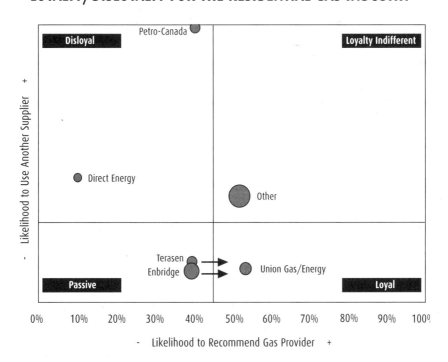

Direct Energy has created the most disloyal customers, followed by Petro-Canada, with a very high likelihood to switch score compared to the rest of the players in the industry. Union Gas/Energy is the company with the most loyal client base, and while customers of Terasen and

Enbridge appear to be passive in Figure 5.10, when customer satisfaction is taken into account, all three companies are below the industry disloyalty average of 80.

The large majority of Canadians do not foresee themselves switching gas providers, and those who do are unsure about which they would switch to. (More than 6 in 10 Canadians said "I don't know" when asked which supplier they would switch to.)

We've already established that as a result of limited choice, consumers become passive. But just because these customers don't currently have alternatives, companies should not relax and stop treating their customers well. As in any industry, there is potential for more competitors coming into the market, and if a good relationship isn't established with these customers, there is significant potential for losing many of them. Planning for the long term as if there are not going to be any changes just doesn't make sense.

_____ Table 5.10 _____

DISLOYALTY INDEX, RESIDENTIAL GAS INDUSTRY

	DISLOYALTY RANKING	DISLOYALTY SCORE	CSAT SCORE	LIKELIHOOD TO RECOMMEND SCORE	LIKELIHOOD TO SWITCH SCORE
Direct Energy	1	113	53	10	−49
Petro-Canada	2	110	61	42	−1
Enbridge	3	74	60	39	−87
Terasen	4	71	52	39	−82
Union Gas/Energy	5	70	72	52	−86

Residential Hydro Industry

The residential hydro industry has even more passive customers than the residential gas industry and, although the satisfaction, likelihood to recommend, and likelihood to switch numbers are all very poor, these customers don't have a choice about which supplier to use.

_____ Figure 5.11 _____

LOYALTY/DISLOYALTY FOR THE RESIDENTIAL HYDRO INDUSTRY

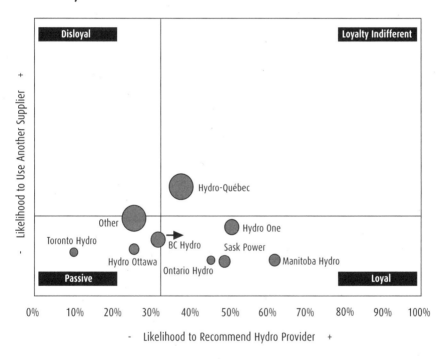

Hydro-Québec, Toronto Hydro, and Hydro Ottawa are above the industry average in terms of disloyalty. (The average is 80.) Manitoba Hydro has the most loyal customers, followed by Sask Power, both with very low likelihood to switch scores, and while customers of BC Hydro appear to be passive due to low likelihood to recommend scores, its overall satisfaction scores give it a lower-than-average disloyalty score. When asked which supplier they would most likely switch to, more than 8 in 10 Canadians said they didn't know, indicating how passive consumers become when they have limited choices.

Again, limited choice results in low likelihood to switch scores. But let's take Ontario as an example, where the government actually deregulated the industry some eight years ago. As we've seen, it can happen. And it will. And although many consumers had become passive and didn't realize that they had choice in hydro providers, the hydro companies in Ontario had to come up with some quick programs to ensure that their customers remained loyal. Even in regulated, monopolistic, or oligopolistic industries, maintaining good client relations is important. The market can change rapidly, and companies need to be proactive about maintaining loyal customers by being loyal themselves.

Table 5.11
DISLOYALTY INDEX, RESIDENTIAL HYDRO INDUSTRY

	DISLOYALTY RANKING	DISLOYALTY SCORE	CSAT SCORE	LIKELIHOOD TO RECOMMEND SCORE	LIKELIHOOD TO SWITCH SCORE
Hydro Ottawa	1	87	55	25	−91
Toronto Hydro	2	86	57	8	−93
Hydro-Québec	3	84	58	38	−60
Ontario Hydro	4	75	61	46	−95
Hydro One	5	74	60	51	−82
BC Hydro	6	72	70	32	−87
Sask Power	7	53	78	49	−95
Manitoba Hydro	8	42	72	63	−94

Quick Serve Restaurant Industry

For QSRs, we've split the industry into two categories: those that specialize in fast food and those that specialize in coffee. Looking at QSRs that specialize in fast food, McDonald's and Burger King have the most disloyal customer base, scoring above the industry average of 75. Companies also above the industry average for disloyalty include Quiznos and Harvey's.

Figure 5.12

LOYALTY/DISLOYALTY FOR
THE QUICK SERVE RESTAURANT INDUSTRY

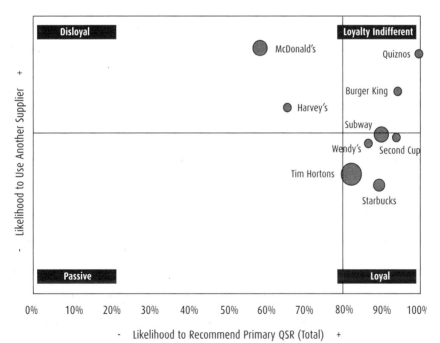

QSRs that specialize in coffee have a fairly loyal customer base and drive the disloyalty average in the industry lower, since consumers generally go out of their way to purchase coffee from their preferred coffee shop. Second Cup appears to have the most disloyal customers according to Table 5.12 (b), due to a higher likelihood to switch score caused by the chain's smaller penetration. However, when customer satisfaction is accounted for, Second Cup actually has the most loyal customers.

Little can be said about maintaining loyal customers in this industry; the coffee retailers are doing it right. And although Tim Hortons is highest in disloyalty among the coffee retailers, the disloyalty scores in this sector are all lower than those of the quick serve restaurants overall. Starbucks and Second Cup have managed to keep their customers coming back by filling the requirements of the niche higher-end coffee drinkers. Tim Hortons is one of the most recognizable Canadian brands, has very high reputation scores, and has the highest penetration of all the coffee retailers in Canada.

—————————————— Table 5.12 (a) ——————————————

DISLOYALTY INDEX, QUICK SERVE RESTAURANT INDUSTRY

	DISLOYALTY RANKING	DISLOYALTY SCORE	CSAT SCORE	LIKELIHOOD TO RECOMMEND SCORE	LIKELIHOOD TO SWITCH SCORE
McDonald's	1	105	65	55	−3
Burger King	2	80	86	92	−18
Quiznos	3	79	70	100	−5
Harvey's	4	78	91	66	−26
Wendy's	5	73	85	87	−43
Subway	6	70	93	90	−36

Table 5.12 (b)
DISLOYALTY INDEX, COFFEE INDUSTRY

	DISLOYALTY RANKING	DISLOYALTY SCORE	CSAT SCORE	LIKELIHOOD TO RECOMMEND SCORE	LIKELIHOOD TO SWITCH SCORE
Tim Hortons	1	67	85	82	−51
Starbucks	2	58	87	90	−56
Second Cup	3	56	99	94	−40

Shipping and Courier Industry

The shipping and courier industry has relatively loyal customers with high satisfaction and likelihood to recommend scores and low likelihood to switch scores. Companies who ship items often have established relationships with a particular supplier and usually only work with one supplier. Customer satisfaction, timeliness, and cost are all important factors in developing a loyal client base in this industry. In addition to the importance of attracting new customers, maintaining a loyal client base is especially important, since customers do have other options.

Figure 5.13

LOYALTY/DISLOYALTY FOR THE SHIPPING AND COURIER INDUSTRY

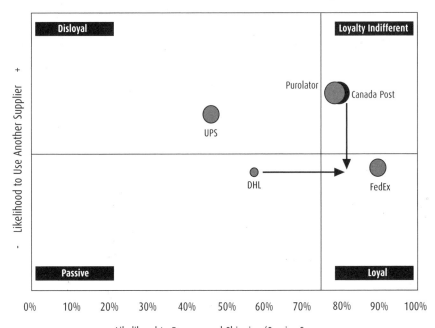

Canada Post has the highest market share in this industry and the second highest score for disloyalty. Although consumers are more likely to use Canada Post, companies that ship often use one of the other suppliers in this industry. UPS has the most disloyal client base, with very poor satisfaction and likelihood to recommend scores and a very high likelihood to switch score. As shown in Figure 5.13 and Table 5.13, FedEx has the most loyal customers in this industry, and while DHL customers appear to be passive, when overall satisfaction is taken into account, they actually turn out to be more loyal. For those Canadians who say they would be inclined to switch to another shipping/courier company, Purolator is the most common choice, followed by FedEx.

While shipping and courier companies have done a good job in assisting their 9 a.m. to 5 p.m. business customers by getting their packages to them the next day, they have not done a good job in satisfying the general consumer who is sending (or receiving) something personally or from a company. When you order something online and it is to be shipped to your house, courier companies often attempt to drop the package off in the middle of the day — when you're at work. Then you get a notice on your door that says "We tried to deliver this to you, but you're not home." So now you have to go to the courier company and pick it up. Hopefully the package isn't too big, and, if it is, hopefully you have a car to go and get it. This is yet another example of company, not consumer, disloyalty.

_____ Table 5.13 _____

DISLOYALTY INDEX, SHIPPING AND COURIER INDUSTRY

	DISLOYALTY RANKING	DISLOYALTY SCORE	CSAT SCORE	LIKELIHOOD TO RECOMMEND SCORE	LIKELIHOOD TO SWITCH SCORE
UPS	1	102	62	46	–32
Canada Post	2	72	84	79	–56
Purolator	3	72	85	78	–25
DHL	4	68	72	58	–56
FedEx	5	58	91	90	–54

Supermarket Industry

The supermarket industry has generally loyal customers, as evidenced by the fact that many Canadians tend to have one grocery store that they shop at most often. In addition to the service experience, product quality, availability, and variety play a big role in maintaining a loyal client base in this industry. With many Canadians attempting to live a healthier lifestyle and looking for natural alternatives (such as organic produce), the availability of these foods is essential in attracting and maintaining these customers.

_____ Figure 5.14 _____

LOYALTY/DISLOYALTY FOR THE SUPERMARKET INDUSTRY

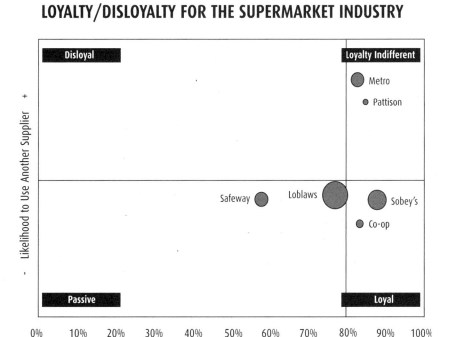

Loblaws, Safeway, Pattison, and Metro are above the industry average of 72 for disloyalty due to lower overall satisfaction and likelihood to recommend scores and, in the case of the Pattison and Metro chains, due to higher likelihood to switch scores. Co-op and Sobey's have the most loyal customers, scoring below the industry average of 72 in terms of disloyalty. Shoppers likely to switch the grocery store they shop at will probably choose Loblaws, followed closely by Sobey's.

Grocery stores have an interesting challenge on their hands. There are many different factors that influence our grocery retailer of choice: Location, prices, product/produce quality and availability, and the service experience are some of the big ones. Most of us, however, have probably not stopped to think as much about the service experience or how we are treated at the supermarket. It is interesting to note that a customer who is purchasing hundreds of dollars worth of groceries has to wait in line, while the person who is buying two items gets to go through an "express checkout." We've become so accustomed to this, none of us questions it. So, you might spend $500 to $1,000 at a grocery store every month, but how loyal is that grocer to you?

_____ Table 5.14 _____
DISLOYALTY INDEX, SUPERMARKET INDUSTRY

	DISLOYALTY RANKING	DISLOYALTY SCORE	CSAT SCORE	LIKELIHOOD TO RECOMMEND SCORE	LIKELIHOOD TO SWITCH SCORE
Metro	1	85	86	84	−12
Pattison	2	80	95	86	−22
Safeway	3	78	82	58	−51
Loblaws	4	74	77	77	−49
Sobey's	5	59	93	89	−52
Co-op	6	59	88	84	−62

Insurance Industry

Overall, the insurance industry has loyal clients. Canadians generally enter into long-term relationships with their insurance companies and rely on them for advice and guidance. However, the way people are treated when they need to make a claim against their policy greatly in-

fluences their loyalty. It can also be argued that we tend to be more passive when it comes to this industry because the process of switching
providers is time-consuming. Calling 10 different insurance companies to
find the one that can offer you the best value for your money is often not
worth the $100 or $200 in potential savings. However, it is important
to note that some insurance companies are making it easier for customers to switch and providing incentives to those who do. The vast
number of competitors in this industry should make these companies
want to develop a more loyal client base. To do that, they have to start
by being more loyal to their customers.

_____ Figure 5.15 _____
LOYALTY/DISLOYALTY FOR THE INSURANCE INDUSTRY

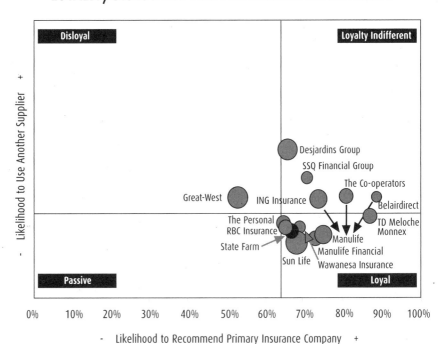

Scores in this industry vary greatly, with a 22-point range in customer satisfaction scores and a 36-point range in likelihood to recommend. The difference in likelihood to switch is even greater, with a 38-point range among the competitors. Considering customer loyalty in the insurance industry, the number of competitors to choose from, and the complex nature of the industry, it is not surprising that the majority of Canadians who would be inclined to switch their primary insurance provider are uncertain about who they would switch to.

_____ Table 5.15 _____

DISLOYALTY INDEX, INSURANCE INDUSTRY

	DISLOYALTY RANKING	DISLOYALTY SCORE	CSAT SCORE	LIKELIHOOD TO RECOMMEND SCORE	LIKELIHOOD TO SWITCH SCORE
Desjardins Group	1	90	75	65	−38
Wawanesa Insurance	2	83	68	68	−71
SSQ Financial Group	3	82	77	70	−50
Great-West	4	77	74	52	−59
RBC Insurance	5	74	72	64	−70
The Personal	6	73	74	64	−69
ING Insurance	7	68	77	73	−59
Sun Life	8	63	83	67	−77
State Farm	9	61	73	66	−72
Manulife Financial	10	61	70	72	−76
TD Meloche Monnex	11	60	85	86	−66
Manulife	12	60	77	74	−74
The Co-operators	13	60	93	80	−58
Belairdirect	14	52	90	88	−58

Retail Pharmacy Industry

Due to the personal relationship that is established with a pharmacist, Canadians tend to be quite loyal to their pharmacies. Shoppers Drug Mart/Pharma Prix has the largest share of the retail pharmacy industry, but their loyalty is not as strong. This may be because Shoppers Drug Mart/Pharma Prix is not only a pharmacy but also provides its customers with many other products, making convenience and price a factor in their disloyalty score.

_____ Figure 5.16 _____
LOYALTY/DISLOYALTY FOR THE RETAIL PHARMACY INDUSTRY

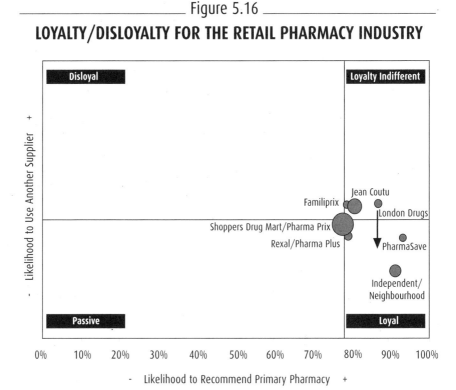

Independent/neighbourhood pharmacies have the most loyal customers in this industry, with a disloyalty score of only 42. Customers of these pharmacies cite very high overall satisfaction, are very likely to recommend, and not likely to switch to another pharmacy. PharmaSave follows closely behind, with a disloyalty score of 46. Independent/neighbourhood pharmacies, PharmaSave, and London Drugs all rank below the industry average of 65 in terms of disloyalty. While primary customers of London Drugs may appear to be loyalty-indifferent because of their higher likelihood to switch, when overall customer satisfaction is accounted for, they are actually quite loyal.

Personal relationships are important in this industry. Even in other studies we've conducted, people are the most satisfied with the independent/neighbourhood pharmacies where they buy their medications. These pharmacists know their clients, help them understand their medications, explain how a medication might interact with other medications they are on, and discuss the side effects of the medications. And although the bigger chain pharmacies have started providing similar services, customers are much more likely to remain loyal to the person they have an established relationship with.

_____ Table 5.16 _____
DISLOYALTY INDEX, RETAIL PHARMACY INDUSTRY

	DISLOYALTY RANKING	DISLOYALTY SCORE	CSAT SCORE	LIKELIHOOD TO RECOMMEND SCORE	LIKELIHOOD TO SWITCH SCORE
Jean Coutu	1	73	93	80	−48
Familiprix	2	71	93	78	−47
Shoppers Drug Mart/ Pharma Prix	3	67	87	77	−56
Rexall/Pharma Plus	4	66	90	78	−61
London Drugs	5	62	92	86	−47
PharmaSave	6	46	94	92	−60
Independent/ Neighbourhood Pharmacies	7	42	98	90	−76

Financial Services Industry

Both Bank of Montreal (BMO) and National Bank of Canada have less than average customer satisfaction and likelihood to recommend scores and the highest likelihood to switch scores. PC Financial and credit unions have the most loyal clientele. Their primary customers are above the industry average in terms of their likelihood to recommend and below the industry average in terms of their likelihood to use another financial institution.

_____ Figure 5.17 _____

LOYALTY/DISLOYALTY FOR THE FINANCIAL SERVICES INDUSTRY

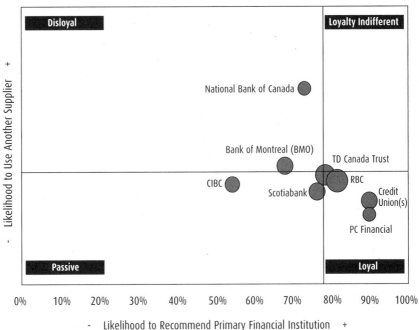

The importance of customer satisfaction to loyalty can be seen in the cases of Scotiabank, TD Canada Trust, and Royal Bank of Canada (RBC). While Figure 5.17 labels Scotiabank's primary customers as passive, when customer satisfaction is accounted for, Scotiabank actually ranks higher than TD and RBC in terms of loyalty. In fact, Scotiabank and TD Canada Trust are below the industry average for disloyalty. (The average is 63.) Figure 5.17 only takes two of the variables into consideration, while the disloyalty index includes customer satisfaction. While Canadians who are inclined to switch financial institutions do not generally know which one they would switch to, TD Canada Trust is the most common choice.

Relationship building is very important in this type of industry. Consumers want to feel secure with the institutions that are holding their savings or investing their money. And who better to discuss your financial situation with than somebody from an institution that is familiar with your portfolio, your assets, your way of life, etc.? The process becomes engaging and more consultative than a simple transaction. As more of us are moving away from visiting our local branches, however, competitors in this industry will have to find different ways of building and maintaining relationships with their clientele.

_____ Table 5.17 _____
DISLOYALTY INDEX, FINANCIAL SERVICES INDUSTRY

	DISLOYALTY RANKING	DISLOYALTY SCORE	CSAT SCORE	LIKELIHOOD TO RECOMMEND SCORE	LIKELIHOOD TO SWITCH SCORE
National Bank of Canada	1	85	75	73	–26
Bank of Montreal (BMO)	2	76	73	68	–54
CIBC	3	75	66	55	–60
Royal Bank of Canada (RBC)	4	63	83	81	–59
TD Canada Trust	5	60	80	78	–56
Scotiabank	6	58	80	76	–64
Credit Unions	7	48	89	90	–68

_____ Table 5.18 _____

DISLOYALTY INDEX, OVERALL COMPANY DISLOYALTY RANKING

	DISLOYALTY RANKING	DISLOYALTY SCORE	CSAT SCORE	LIKELIHOOD TO RECOMMEND SCORE	LIKELIHOOD TO SWITCH SCORE
Air Transat	1	126	63	50	32
Air Canada	2	125	52	49	31
Bell Mobility	3	114	52	33	−25
Direct Energy	4	113	53	10	−49
Future Shop	5	111	66	60	13
Petro-Canada (Residential Gas)	6	110	61	42	−1
American Express	7	110	74	79	−49
Source by Circuit City	8	107	71	55	14
Bell (Cable)	9	106	59	45	−33
McDonald's	10	105	65	55	−3
TELUS Wireless	11	104	55	43	−44
TD Visa	12	104	69	61	−14
Esso	13	103	66	48	−17
UPS	14	102	62	46	−32
Reno Depot	15	99	75	76	12
Rogers Wireless	16	99	58	50	−46
BMO MasterCard	17	96	82	70	−8
Canadian Tire	18	96	71	73	−21
Shell	19	94	72	62	−15
Home Depot	20	94	74	73	−15
Best Buy	21	93	73	78	−7
RBC Visa	22	93	88	66	−16
The Bay	23	93	68	66	−36
Rona	24	93	73	65	−32
Petro-Canada	25	93	74	55	−23

Table 5.18
DISLOYALTY INDEX, OVERALL COMPANY DISLOYALTY RANKING

	DISLOYALTY RANKING	DISLOYALTY SCORE	CSAT SCORE	LIKELIHOOD TO RECOMMEND SCORE	LIKELIHOOD TO SWITCH SCORE
PC MasterCard	26	93	84	79	−25
Walmart	27	92	68	64	−36
Rogers (Cable)	28	92	61	50	−45
Desjardins Group	29	90	75	65	−38
Hydro Ottawa	30	87	55	25	−91
Toronto Hydro	31	86	57	8	−93
Metro	32	85	86	84	−12
National Bank of Canada	33	85	75	73	−26
Home Hardware	34	84	65	68	−27
Zellers	35˙	84	78	77	−49
Hydro-Québec	36	84	58	38	−60
Scotiabank Visa	37	84	77	80	18
Wawanesa Insurance	38	83	68	68	−71
SSQ Financial Group	39	82	77	70	−50
Videotron	40	82	80	68	−43
Fido	41	81	68	59	−60
Pattison	42	80	95	86	−22
Burger King	43	80	86	92	−18
Quiznos	44	79	70	100	−5
Harvey's	45	78	91	66	−26
Safeway	46	78	82	58	−51
Shaw (Star Choice)	47	77	68	73	−58
Great-West	48	77	74	52	−59
Bank of Montreal (BMO)	49	76	73	68	−54

_____ Table 5.18 _____
DISLOYALTY INDEX, OVERALL COMPANY DISLOYALTY RANKING

	DISLOYALTY RANKING	DISLOYALTY SCORE	CSAT SCORE	LIKELIHOOD TO RECOMMEND SCORE	LIKELIHOOD TO SWITCH SCORE
Ontario Hydro	50	75	61	46	−95
CIBC	51	75	66	55	−60
Enbridge	52	74	60	39	−87
Hydro One	53	74	60	51	−82
Loblaws	54	74	77	77	−49
RBC Insurance	55	74	72	64	−70
Jean Coutu	56	73	93	80	−48
The Personal	57	73	74	64	−69
Wendy's	58	73	85	87	−43
Canada Post	59	72	84	79	−56
Purolator	60	72	85	78	−25
BC Hydro	61	72	70	32	−87
Terasen	62	71	52	39	−82
Familiprix	63	71	93	78	−47
Subway	64	70	93	90	−36
Sears	65	70	84	73	−40
Union Gas/Energy	66	70	72	52	−86
ING Insurance	67	68	77	73	−59
DHL	68	68	72	58	−56
Shoppers Drug Mart/Pharma Prix	69	67	87	77	−56
Tim Hortons	70	67	85	82	−51
Rexall/Pharma Plus	71	66	90	78	−61
Costco/Price Club	72	66	81	82	−66
Cogeco	73	65	80	85	−69
Sun Life	74	63	83	67	−77

Table 5.18
DISLOYALTY INDEX, OVERALL COMPANY DISLOYALTY RANKING

	DISLOYALTY RANKING	DISLOYALTY SCORE	CSAT SCORE	LIKELIHOOD TO RECOMMEND SCORE	LIKELIHOOD TO SWITCH SCORE
Via Rail	75	63	81	79	−57
RBC	76	63	83	81	−59
London Drugs	77	62	92	86	−47
State Farm	78	61	73	66	−72
Manulife Financial	79	61	70	72	−76
Virgin Mobile	80	60	73	76	−66
TD Meloche Monnex	81	60	85	86	−66
Manulife	82	60	77	74	−74
TD Canada Trust	83	60	80	78	−56
The Co-operators	84	60	93	80	−58
Sobey's	85	59	93	89	−52
Co-op	86	59	88	84	−62
FedEx	87	58	91	90	−54
Starbucks	88	58	87	90	−56
Scotiabank	89	58	80	76	−64
Second Cup	90	56	99	94	−40
WestJet	91	55	91	98	−35
Sask Power	92	53	78	49	−95
Belairdirect	93	52	90	88	−58
Credit Unions	94	48	89	90	−68
PC Financial	95	47	90	90	−74
PharmaSave	96	45	94	92	−60
Manitoba Hydro	97	42	78	63	−94
Independent/ Neighbourhood Pharmacy	98	41	98	90	−76

REFERENCES AND BIBLIOGRAPHY

Bloemer, José, and Ko de Ruyter. 1998. "On the Relationship Between Store Image, Store Satisfaction and Store Loyalty." *European Journal of Marketing* 32 (5/6): 499–513.

Brown, George H. 1952. "Brand Loyalty–Fact or Fiction?" *Advertising Age* 23 (9): 52–55.

Cunningham, Ross M. 1956. "Brand Loyalty–What, Where, How Much?" *Harvard Business Review* 34 (1): 116–128.

Day, George S. 1969. "A Two-Dimensional Concept of Brand Loyalty." *Journal of Advertising Research* 9 (3): 29–35.

Duffer, Jean, and Jean-Louis Moulins. 1989. "La relation entre la satisfaction du consommateur et sa fidélité à la marque: Un examen critique." *Recherche et applications en marketing* 4 (2): 21–36.

Engel, James F., and Roger D. Blackwell. 1982. *Consumer Behavior.* 4th ed. Toronto: Dryden Press.

The Free Dictionary by Farlex. 2003. "Conative" (from *The American Heritage Dictionary of the English Language*, 4th ed., Houghton Mifflin Company, 2000 and 2003), at www.thefreedictionary.com/Conative (accessed 27 April 2009).

Helgesen, Oyvind. 2006. "Are Loyal Customers Profitable? Customer Satisfaction, Customer (Action) Loyalty and Customer Profitability at the Individual Level." *Journal of Marketing Management* 22: 245–66.

Hill, Nigel, and Jim Alexander. 2000. *Handbook of Customer Satisfaction and Loyalty Measurement.* 2nd ed. Aldershot, UK: Gower Publishing.

Howard, John, and Jagdish, Sheth. 1969. The Theory of Buyer Behaviour. New York: John Wiley & Sons.

Jacoby, Jacob. 1971. "A Model of Multi-brand Loyalty." *Journal of Advertising Research* 11: 25–31.

Jacoby, Jacob, and Robert W. Chestnut. 1978. *Brand Loyalty Measurement and Management.* New York: John Wiley & Sons.

Jacoby, Jacob, and David B. Kyner. 1973. "Brand Loyalty vs. Repeat Purchasing Behavior." *Journal of Marketing Research* 10: 1–9.

Johnson, Michael D., Tor W. Andreassen, Line Lervik, and Jaesung Cha. 2001. "The Evolution and Future of National Customer Satisfaction Index Models." *Journal of Economic Psychology* 22: 217–245.

Keiningham, Timothy L., Bruce Cooil, Lerzan Aksoy, Tor W. Andreassen, and Jay Weiner. 2007. "The Value of Different Customer Satisfaction and Loyalty Metrics in Predicting Customer Retention, Recommendation and Share of Wallet." *Managing Service Quality* 17 (4).

Khatibi, Abod Ali, Hishamuddin Ismail, and Venu Thygarajan. 2002. "What Drives Customer Loyalty: An Analysis from the Telecommunications Industry." *Journal of Targeting* 11 (1): 34–44.

Macintosh, Gerrard, and Lawrence S. Lockshin. 1997. "Retail Relationships and Store Loyalty: A Multi-Level Perspective." *International Journal of Research in Marketing* 14 (12): 487–97.

Martinez Garcia, Jose Antonio, and Laura Martinez Caro. 2008. "Building Better Causal Models to Measure the Relationship Between Attitudes and Customer Loyalty." *International Journal of Market Research* 50 (4): 437–47.

The Merriam-Webster Online Dictionary. 2009. "Conative" at www.merriam-webster.com/dictionary/conative (accessed 27 April 2009).

Mittal, Vikas, and Wagner A. Kamakura. 2001. "Satisfaction, Repurchase Intent, and Repurchase Behavior: Investigating the Moderating Effect of Customer Characteristics." *Journal of Marketing Research* 37: 131–142.

Morgan, Neil A., and Lopo Leotte Rego. 2006. "The Value of Different Customer Satisfaction and Loyalty Metrics in Predicting Business Performance." *Marketing Science* 25 (5): 426–39.

Oliver, Richard L. 1999. "Whence Consumer Loyalty?" *Journal of Marketing* 63: 33-44.

Reichheld, Fred. 2006. *The Ultimate Question: Driving Good Profits and True Growth.* Boston: Harvard Business School Press.

Szymanski, David M., and David H. Henard. 2001. "Customer Satisfaction: A Meta-Analysis of the Empirical Evidence." *Journal of the Academy of Marketing Science* 29 (1): 16–35.

Taylor, Steven, and Thomas Baker. 1994. "An Assessment of the Relationship Between Service Quality and Customer Satisfaction in the Formation of Consumers' Purchase Intentions." *Journal of Retailing* 70 (2): 163–178.

Chapter 6

THE EMPOWERED CONSUMER

Sylvain Sénécal, PhD, HEC Montréal

Introduction

A revolution is under way. For some time now, consumers have had easy access to online information sources providing useful information in order to help them make more informed decisions and get the service they expect from companies. These sources are generally other consumers who use the Internet (through online communities, blogs, etc.) to voice their opinions and share their advice. Welcome to the world of empowered consumers!

First, this chapter shows that consumers have always had power, how companies can empower consumers, and, most important, how the Internet empowers consumers. Second, it presents the results of a nationwide survey assessing whether and how Canadians are empowered by the Internet. Finally, it presents how leading companies use the Internet as not only a tool to empower consumers but also a marketing research tool to take the pulse of consumers and try to service them in better ways.

What Is Consumer Empowerment?

Empowered consumers are consumers who have control over the product-related information they are exposed to or over their interactions with companies while performing consumption activities. For instance, a consumer using a digital video recorder (DVR) or personal video recorder (PVR) can watch his or her favourite television shows without commercial interruptions. Another consumer may use the Internet to find out what other consumers think about a specific product before buying it. That consumer can seek unbiased product information from other consumers on third-party websites such as Epinions.com. What do these two consumers have in common? They are empowered. They have a certain level of control over their interaction with product-related information. As we will see, consumers have always had power over companies, but technology, and specifically the Internet, gives consumer empowerment a whole new meaning.

Business as Usual: Consumers Have Always Had Power

Consumers have always had power over some of the steps in the purchasing process. Let's see how this has worked traditionally:

The consumer's decision-making process

Consumers go through a decision-making process when purchasing products and services. This process usually starts with the recognition of a problem (e.g., I would like to listen to music while I am jogging), then moves to the information search stage. (What do I know about portable music devices? What products and brands are offered on the market? Do I know an expert on such devices?) Once the information is gathered, an evaluation of the available products is made and an intention to purchase is formed (e.g., I will buy the silver iPod Nano at Circuit City). Then, the product is purchased. Following the purchase, the product is used and evaluated.

Figure 6.1
THE CONSUMER'S DECISION-MAKING PROCESS

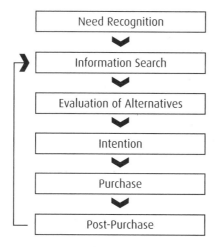

Traditionally, consumers have had power over three of these decision-making stages: problem recognition, purchase, and post-purchase. And the goal of advertising is to capture the attention of as many potential customers as possible in order to convince them that the advertised product or service is the best product or service on the market to fulfill their need. Since consumers know that most of the advertisements in their environment are not relevant to them, they filter out most of them and only process those that are relevant. Thus, they consciously (e.g., by muting or using DVR) or unconsciously (e.g., by not paying attention to the top of webpages, where banner ads are usually located) decide to be exposed or not and, if exposed, to process the advertisements or not. Thus, even if they are bombarded every day by thousands of advertisements, consumers process a very small fraction of them. They primarily process advertisements they perceive as being currently relevant to them. Even though consumers often say that they are overwhelmed with advertising stimuli in their daily lives, they are, in fact, naturally equipped to deal with these stimuli. Even if they don't really feel that they are empowered at this stage of the decision-making process, they are actually in control of the information they process.

Along with this decision-making process, one stage that is unarguably empowering for consumers is the purchasing stage. At this stage, the consumer chooses one product over other competing products. Obviously, this step is the most critical for companies, since it directly affects their sales and profits. Consumers have a lot of power over companies just by deciding or not deciding to buy a given product. This power has always been present in the marketplace. And certain products have achieved impressive sales figures (e.g., Microsoft Office, VHS recorders) while others have disappeared (e.g., Netscape, Beta recorders) — all as a result of consumer choice.

Another stage at which consumers are traditionally empowered is the post-purchase stage, when they consume and eventually evaluate the product they have bought. During this evaluation stage, they determine their satisfaction level. If they are satisfied, they will mention it to fellow consumers and potentially repurchase the product. If they are not, they will usually mention it to even more fellow consumers and will not repurchase the product. In addition, unsatisfied consumers may also officially complain to companies or other agencies (e.g., governmental agencies, retailers, or manufacturers). Accordingly, consumers are naturally empowered: They do not need the help of companies to be in a position of power, since they are the ones ultimately deciding to buy, or not to buy, a product or service.

However, this traditional level of empowerment is not sufficient to ensure making good purchase decisions. In fact, research shows that for some products and services, consumers are so powerless that many subcontract their decisions to sales representatives (Zeithaml 1982; Miyazaki, Sprott, and Manning 2000). In these cases, consumers feel that they did not have the capability or motivation to find the best product, but they know they have to fulfill their needs. The point here is that since they are not empowered in all their decision-making stages (e.g., information search and evaluation of alternatives), they may end up buying products and services that do not completely fulfill their needs. In many instances, the information asymmetry between companies and consumers is quite significant — and, of course, in favour of companies. For instance, in the past it was difficult for consumers to know if their travel agent was suggesting the best route, carrier, or price, since they had no way to verify the information. They had to either simply trust their agent or visit multiple travel agencies in an effort to gather the information to make a good decision. Nowadays, online travel agencies, such as Expedia.com, empower consumers by allowing them to search for the information themselves.

Business as Usual, but with a Twist: Companies Empower Consumers

By empowering consumers, companies such as Expedia.com hope that their customers' satisfaction levels will increase. Over the years, companies in various industries have developed essentially three ways to empower their customers:

1. Offer a larger product assortment and options.

2. Provide more information.

3. Improve communication among or with consumers.

Offer a larger product assortment and options

When they are offered a larger assortment of products, consumers can feel empowered by their increased range of choice (i.e., more product lines and models). In addition, by giving more product-related options, companies also empower consumers. For instance, many car manufacturers offer option bundles (e.g., touring) as well as à la carte options (e.g., entertainment systems) to consumers. By providing this flexibility, they empower consumers, who can assemble a group of options or bundles to satisfy their needs. However, consumers can also be overwhelmed by too many models and options. In this case, companies can couple their larger assortment offers with information and tools to help consumers arrive at an optimal decision.

Provide more information

To improve the feeling of empowerment, companies can also provide consumers with information to make better-informed purchase decisions. First, companies can provide better product information, which in turn should help consumers make better decisions. For instance, on its website, the cosmetics company Maybelline New York offers consumers the opportunity to see the different colours of its products in photos of real models. In addition, companies can equip consumers with complementary information, such as buying guides and tips that will help them correctly identify the best products for them. For instance, Maybelline New York offers consumers "How to" videos on its website to show how to use their products.

Offering greater information and complementary information may satisfy some consumers, but, as mentioned, others may feel overwhelmed. In such cases, companies can also provide consumers with product-comparison tools to help them make better decisions. Product-comparison tools can be quite effective. For instance, consumer research found that when consumers are provided with a product unit price (e.g., $0.30 per litre) compared to just a raw product price (e.g., $2.99), they select different products and end up spending less (Zeithaml 1982; Miyazaki, Sprott, and Manning 2000). So providing a comparison tool empowers consumers and helps them to make better-informed decisions. On the Internet, many companies provide a product-comparison matrix in order to help consumers compare alternatives. For instance, the website of National Bank of Canada (nbc.ca) offers a credit card comparison tool for consumers to easily compare the various attributes of each card they are considering. Some innovative companies are empowering consumers by providing transparent information about their competitors' offers. For instance, the insurance company Belairdirect (belairdirect.com) is offering consumers a tool to compare its insurance price quotes with price quotes of competitors on its website, using third-party information.

So by providing more information, companies empower consumers in their information search stage, and by providing tools to compare products, they empower consumers in their evaluation of alternatives stage.

Improve communication among or with consumers

Companies can also empower consumers by giving them the means to exchange information with the company or among themselves. Giving consumers convenient access to companies makes consumers feel that they are valued and that they can be heard. For instance, the customer relationship company Salesforce.com has set up a website where its customers can suggest new features to include in coming releases of its products. In addition, customers vote on these suggestions in order for Salesforce.com to easily identify those features that would be the most appreciated by customers. Some companies also support communication between consumers. This ranges from posting customers' testimonials on company websites to sponsoring virtual communities where consumers can interact with one another. For instance, Dell operates a virtual community where customers can discuss issues pertaining to Dell's products.

Giving consumers better means of communication empowers them at multiple stages in their decision-making process, since communication with companies or among consumers can be useful at various stages.

The Ongoing Revolution: The Internet Empowers Consumers

The Internet is primarily a communications network. It can be used for mass communication (e.g., websites) or personal communication (e.g., email), and it can be used by both individuals and companies alike. Individuals and companies have a long history of using personal communication modes as a means to communicate with other companies or individuals (e.g., mail, phone, fax). Companies are also well versed in the use of mass media to communicate with other companies and with individual consumers (e.g., print, TV, radio). What is new in the use of mass communication by consumers is their ability to communicate either among themselves or with companies (i.e., the information can now flow in all directions rather than just from the company to the consumer).

_____ Table 6.1 _____

COMMUNICATIONS MATRIX BETWEEN INDIVIDUALS AND COMPANIES

	PERSONAL COMMUNICATION	MASS COMMUNICATION
Individuals → Companies	Traditional	Novel
Companies → Individuals	Traditional	Traditional
Individuals → Individuals	Traditional	Novel
Companies → Companies	Traditional	Traditional

For consumers, it is quite novel to have relatively easy access to mass media (e.g., YouTube, Flickr, Facebook, Blogger, Wikipedia). This is what has been referred to as Web 2.0, participative Web, social Web, or user-generated content (UGC). Consumers can now use the Internet to generate various types of content in various formats and communicate this content to individuals and companies using means of mass communication. UGC can take various forms: text, audio, video, or virtual (adapted from OECD 2007).

Table 6.2
TYPES OF UGC CONTENT

TYPE OF CONTENT	EXAMPLES
Audio	Podcasting, music
Rating	Movie ratings, voting
Text	Blogs, forums, newsgroups
Video	Video blogs, music videos
Virtual	Virtual goods

In addition, this content can be distributed on various platforms: blogs, wikis, sites with user-feedback functionalities (e.g., Amazon), group-based aggregation sites (e.g., Digg, Delicious), podcasting sites (e.g., iTunes, FeedBurner), social-networking sites (e.g., MySpace, Facebook), virtual worlds (e.g., Second Life, Club Penguin), and file-sharing sites (e.g., Digital Media Project, BitTorrent) (OECD 2007).

Hence, individual consumers can now contribute a wide variety of content to a variety of platforms. When the content is related to products and services offered by companies, consumers using these platforms can have a major impact on the attitudes, intentions, and behaviours of fellow consumers. Thus, using technology, consumers are more empowered than before. Consumers can use technology at different stages of their decision-making process in order to make better consumption decisions. The following hypothetical example illustrates how a consumer can be empowered by the Internet in most stages of the decision-making process.

The digital camera example

At the information search stage, the consumer can use the Internet to gather information about products and also about important product attributes to consider while choosing a product within a product category. For instance, if a woman is shopping for a digital camera, she could go to the CNET website (cnet.com) to learn about digital cameras (see, e.g., the buying guide) and also consult reviews by experts (in both text and video format) and fellow consumers (in text format) on specific models. She could also chat with fellow consumers through the digital camera forum. In addition, she could look for blog posts, videos, groups, forums, and product rating sites for digital cameras to gather more product information. And none of the information she gathers would come from a retailer or manufacturer of digital cameras.

Once enough information is gathered, she reaches the next stage of the decision-making process where she evaluates the different models offered in order to decide which product to buy and where to buy it. At this stage, she could use the comparison matrix of the CNET website to compare products.

She could also go to MyProductAdvisor.com (myproductadvisor.com) to fill out a questionnaire about her needs and preferences about digital cameras and get a personalized product recommendation. On each of these sites, she could also compare retailers' prices and select from which retailer she would like to buy the product she has chosen.

All of these activities are performed on third-party websites.

Finally, she would go to a retailer's website to order the product. But even on this website, she could be influenced by content generated by fellow consumers, since many retailers' websites carry customer reviews of the products. She could also be exposed to content from other consumers while looking at the retailer's product page, without the knowledge of the retailer. For instance, if she had her Weblin avatar (weblin.com), she could meet fellow consumers' avatars who are looking at the retailer's product page at the same time and chat with them about the product's features and price, prices at other retailers, etc.

Once the product is bought, received, and used, she could go back online to share her product evaluation (positive, neutral, or negative) using different formats on different UGC platforms (e.g., posts on CNET, video on YouTube, reviews on the retailer's website, a review and pictures on her blog or on her Facebook page). If, for some reason, she would like to voice a complaint directly to the manufacturer, she could use the Get2Human (get2human.com) website to find out how to reach a real person without wasting time in the manufacturer's phone system. If this interaction with the manufacturer is not to her satisfaction, she could also join online pressure groups (e.g., homedepotsucks.org).

This example of a consumer buying a digital camera illustrates that consumers can use many types of UGC at various steps of their decision-making process. In addition, it shows that UGC is, for the most part, located on third-party websites. Thus, empowered consumers, if they want to, can go through most of their decision-making process without directly interacting with retailers or manufacturers. This example illustrates the decision-making process of a highly empowered hypothetical consumer.

But do real consumers actually feel empowered by the Internet?

Do Canadians Feel Empowered by the Internet?

In June 2008, Leger Marketing conducted an online survey to assess the level of empowerment Canadians perceived while using the Internet. A sample composed of 1,502 participants was asked a series of questions on how the Internet empowers them.

Based on the survey results (see Table 6.3), it is quite clear that Canadians feel empowered by the Internet. They mostly agreed that on the Internet, they can either control their exposure to companies (Q1), find information and tools to make better decisions (Q2, Q3), or access tools to make their voices heard (Q4, Q5).

_____ Table 6.3 _____
EMPOWERMENT DESCRIPTIVE RESULTS

QUESTION	MEAN	MEDIAN
Q1. The Internet gives me more control over my exposure to advertisements compared to other media.	6.4	7
Q2. Using the Internet, I can find products and services that I cannot find in local stores.	7.4	8
Q3. Internet tools such as comparison-shopping websites and product information posted online by other consumers help me make better purchase decisions.	6.9	7
Q4. On the Internet, it is easy to voice my opinion on products and services to other consumers, retailers, and manufacturers.	7.1	8
Q5. Using the Internet, consumers can join forces and get companies to respect their promises.	6.3	7
Empowerment Index (mean of the five questions above)	**6.8**	**7**

Note: Answers were given an a scale from 1 to 10 where 1 means "totally disagree" and 10 means "totally agree"; N = 1,502.

These five questions were averaged to form an Empowerment Index, which was used to compare respondents in terms of their demographic profile (sex, age, education, occupation, language, and province).

First, results showed that men felt significantly more empowered by the Internet than did women (with means of 7.0 for men and 6.7 for women).

Second, as shown in Figure 6.2, not all age groups felt equally empowered by the Internet. Roughly, empowerment slowly increased until the mid-40s and then started a somewhat rapid decline. It seems likely that as younger groups grow older, the Empowerment Index will increase for the older age groups.

Figure 6.2

EMPOWERMENT AND AGE

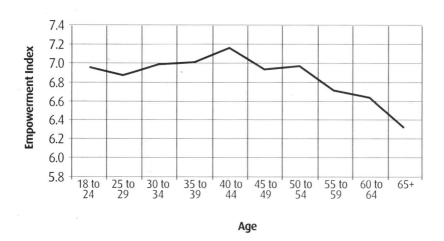

Third, results (see Figure 6.3) showed that gross household income influenced people's perception of their empowerment by the Internet. With the exception of the less than $19,999 income level, empowerment increased with gross household income level. Interestingly, the less than

$19,999 income level reached the highest empowerment level of all income brackets. However, since this income level had the highest concentration of students and homemakers (35%), this result is not surprising.

_____ Figure 6.3 _____
EMPOWERMENT AND GROSS HOUSEHOLD INCOME

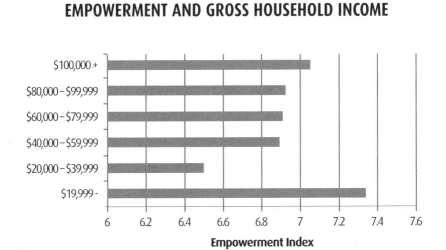

Fourth, the type of occupation also influenced Canadians' perception of Internet empowerment. (See Figure 6.4.) As one might expect, science and technology workers felt more empowered than other Canadians. And manual labourers were those with the lowest perceived empowerment level.

_____ Figure 6.4 _____
EMPOWERMENT AND OCCUPATION

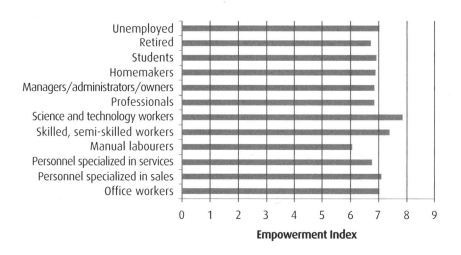

Fifth, a significant difference was found between respondents using French as their usual language and respondents using either English or another language as their usual language. (See Figure 6.5.) Since most websites are in English, the language barrier may play a role in empowering consumers.

_____ Figure 6.5 _____
EMPOWERMENT AND LANGUAGE

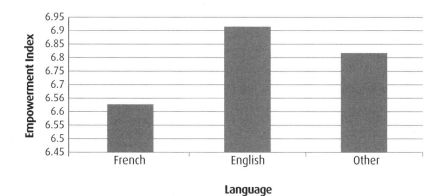

Finally, results suggested that respondents from two provinces felt less empowered by the Internet than those of other provinces. (See Figure 6.6.) As mentioned, the language barrier may play a role in the empowerment of respondents from Quebec. However, it is more surprising that Albertans felt less empowered than other Canadians. Respondents from British Columbia felt the most empowered by the Internet.

Figure 6.6
EMPOWERMENT AND PROVINCE

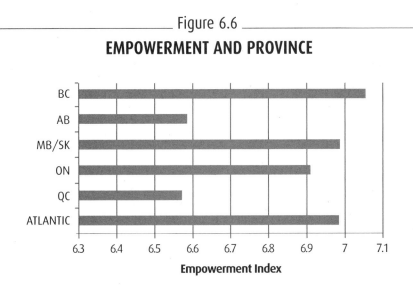

Empowerment Index

What Can Companies Do About Consumer Empowerment?

Since most Canadian Internet users feel empowered by the Internet, companies must recognize this evolving business landscape and adapt their strategies. Companies should at least use UGC to conduct basic marketing research activities to understand how their brands are perceived by online consumers. More proactive companies can also use the Internet's interactive characteristics to innovate while performing a broader range of marketing activities such as marketing research, advertising and branding, and customer support.

Marketing research

Companies can use UGC to learn about consumers' attitudes and perceptions towards their brands and their competitors' brands. Companies can monitor their brands by mining Internet data, such as blogs and consumers' posts on community websites. Social Web monitoring companies such as Exvisu, Radian6, Scout Labs, and Umbria all offer services to monitor what Internet users mention about brands. For instance, Dell monitored the Internet after a blogger mentioned that Dell was working on the release of a mini notebook (the Inspiron 910) (Radian6 n.d.). For four months before the product's actual release, Dell used UGC to fine-tune it (features, pricing, positioning) and measure the buzz surrounding its release.

Advertising and branding

Companies can also incorporate UGC in their advertising and branding efforts. In these activities using UGC, consumers, rather than the companies, are conveying the brand's message to fellow consumers. For instance, Frito Lay's Doritos brand has been successfully using this strategy for the past several years with a contest in which consumers can submit a 30-second TV commercial featuring Doritos ("Doritos Presents" 2008). The commercial that gets the most votes from other consumers is aired during the Super Bowl, and the consumer who created the commercial wins $1 million. Since the winner is not revealed before his or her commercial is aired, this contest succeeds in creating a buzz not only before but also during and even after the Super Bowl, which gives Doritos a lot of media coverage. Chevrolet also used a similar strategy to reach college students in order to promote its Aveo model. In 2006, it created the "Chevy Aveo Livin' Large Campus Challenge" in which pairs of students on seven college campuses had to spend a week living in a Chevy Aveo and post videos on the Aveo website. In order to win the challenge, the participants who created the video with the most votes won a Chevy Aveo. In subsequent years, Chevrolet ran different versions of the contest ("About Livin' Large" 2009).

Customer support

Companies can also use UGC in their customer support activities. For instance, setting up a forum where consumers can help one another solve problems and exchange information about the company's products can be beneficial for the company. Dell has been a pioneer of this technique, setting up online communities such as Direct2Dell, where customers help one another through customer support forums. This forum has grown to 4 million posts, of which about 25% are answers to questions posted by other customers (Bernoff and Li 2008). It must to be noted that such efforts potentially have important cost-saving effects for companies and can also be used to support marketing research activities. For instance, Dell, like Salesforce.com, has launched an idea community section where customers can suggest ideas for new product development. This initiative has led to the development of a line of Dell computers running on the Linux operating system (Bernoff and Li 2008).

Conclusion

In going through their decision-making process when shopping for a product, consumers need information in order to make good purchase decisions. Traditionally, most of the relevant information was held and disseminated by companies (i.e., advocate information sources). Since consumers know that this information can sometimes be biased in favour of companies, they also seek information from relatives, friends, and independent experts (i.e., independent information sources) in order to get a more balanced and objective picture of the situation.

Before the advent of the Internet, getting product information from independent information sources could be challenging for consumers. These sources were usually more limited in number, time consuming to consult, and difficult to reach. But with the Internet and its current wave of UGC, many of these difficulties disappeared.

Furthermore, the advent of the Internet also increased the amount of information available to consumers from advocate sources (corporate websites, retailer websites, etc.).

Thus, consumers are empowered by using the Internet. They are empowered not only because there is more information available but also because there are services that can help them objectively filter this information to confidently make better buying decisions. In addition to helping consumers making better product choices, the Internet can help them get their voices heard by companies after they have bought a product.

Companies must be aware of this empowerment shift and adapt their strategies. As mentioned, they should at least use UGC to listen in and gain insight into what consumers think of their brands. As demonstrated in this chapter, there are more and more examples of companies creatively using UGC to connect with their target segments while performing various marketing activities. These initiatives should continue to grow, and companies that pursue them should develop stronger relationships with their customers. In turn, this should translate into increased satisfaction, loyalty, sales, and profits.

REFERENCES

"About Livin' Large," Chevrolet Aveo Livin' Large home page at http://www.aveolivinlarge.com/pages/about.php, 2009 (accessed 6 May 2009).

Bernoff, Josh, and Charlene Li. 2008. "Harnessing the Power of the Oh-So-Social Web." *MIT Sloan Management Review* 49 (3): 36–42.

"Doritos Presents Crash the Super Bowl," contest website at http://www.crashthesuperbowl.com, 2008 (accessed 6 May 2009).

Miyazaki, A.D., D.E. Sprott, and K.C. Manning. 2000. "Unit Prices in Retail Shelf Labels: An Assessment of Information Prominence." *Journal of Retailing* 76 (1): 93–112.

OECD (Organisation for Economic Co-operation and Development). 2007. *Participative Web and User-Created Content: Web 2.0, Wikis and Social Networking.* Paris: OECD. Available online at http://www.biac.org/members/iccp/mtg/2008-06-seoul-min/9307031E.pdf (accessed 5 May 2009).

Radian6. n.d. "Dell: Free-Range Marketing: Business Case: Product Launch for the Inspiron 910 (Mini 9)," online at http://www.radian6.com/blog/wp-content/uploads/2008/11/dell_lo.pdf (accessed 5 May 2009).

Zeithaml, V.A. 1982. "Consumer Response to In-Store Price Information Environments." *Journal of Consumer Research* 8 (4): 357–69.

Chapter 7

SOCIAL DIALOGUE AND PUBLIC PARTICIPATION: A NEW ERA OF SUSTAINABLE DEVELOPMENT AND RESPONSIBLE ORGANIZATIONS

Solange Tremblay, MA, Université du Québec à Montréal

Guy Lachapelle, PhD, Concordia University

The need for organizations in both public and private sectors to behave in a socially responsible way is becoming a generalized requirement of society.

(International Organization for Standardization/ISO 2008)

If, since the end of the Second World War, companies have been at the heart of the great transformations experienced by industrial society, playing a pivotal role in creating wealth and participating in economic competitiveness, the contract that binds them implicitly with the rest of society is increasingly being questioned. In fact, many groups are asking that they account for their business activities as a whole and demonstrate social responsibility.

The association Business for Social Responsibility (BSR) — a global network of more than 250 companies — contends the following:

Today's business landscape requires that companies navigate a complex and evolving set of economic, environmental and social challenges and address stakeholder demands for greater trans-

parency, accountability and responsibility. These factors affect all aspects of business operations — from supply chain to marketplace and from employee productivity to investor return.

To compete successfully, a company needs to develop responsible business policies and practices and make them an integral part of its mission, values, strategy and operations.

As evidence of the new values that are taking root in the public and social arenas, the very notion of development is being redefined and a new concept has appeared in the public discourse: sustainable development. Moving away from an orientation only geared towards economic growth, it takes into account all human activity — environmental, social, and economic. Placing the human being at the heart of development, sustainable development refers to a global societal project that aims for the social and individual well-being of populations planet-wide. Social responsibility, for its part, concerns the participation of various organizations in this project by incorporating sustainable development values in all of their policies and practices. "It is futile to argue […] that a business has only one responsibility: economic performance," states Peter Drucker. "The demand for socially responsible organizations will not go away; rather, it will widen." (Drucker 1995)

In fact, sustainable development is literally everywhere. Every conference program and forum discussion includes the topic. Over the past 20 years, a growing community has embraced its values. Laws have been enacted. Certifications and standards have been created. National campaigns have worked to build awareness. Its universal values have literally swept the planet, creating a strong wave of sympathy. Any private or public sector organization that has been slow to interpret and respond to the signs is now feeling the heat.

Today's citizens are increasingly well informed and discerning and making their voices heard. More and more, they express criticism about their governments, the governance of society's institutions, and the activities of corporations. They interpret the world around them from multiple perspectives, based on their different statuses. One is the social status conferred by their current role — consumer, client, taxpayer, voter. Another is occupational status — worker, retiree, student, homemaker, unemployed person. The formal and informal groups to which they belong, based on culture, language, or residential community, constitute multiple forums in which they can exchange information and express opinions. With today's explosion of communication channels and the power of the mouse click and camera phone, we have most definitely entered the "everyone's a journalist" era, to borrow d'Almeida's expression (d'Almeida 2007). Citizens have become major players who increasingly influence corporate agendas and actively participate in the transformation of social values.

As some big organizations play catch-up and scramble to ramp up their sustainability initiatives, it is not surprising to see a proliferation of grassroots and monitoring groups watching them and citizens who are striving to influence them on these issues. Many question the degree and sincerity of the commitment championed by these newly converted organizations. They wonder whether they are looking at true sustainable development projects, green masquerades, or cosmetic fixes. With the spread of "greenwashing," how are citizens reacting to corporate discourse and the attempts to seduce them?

The "passive citizen" and the "loyal consumer" are things of the past. The same can be said of "employee loyalty" as we once knew it — rare is the employee today who remains loyal to a single employer during his or her entire career. The face of the "citizen" is being redrawn.

A survey of 1,502 adults across Canada in July 2008 conducted by Leger Marketing provides interesting information to that effect.

An Increasingly Selective Workforce

The survey shows that if respondents were able to select their employers based on sustainability values, more than 70% would choose an organization committed to sustainable business. (See Figure 7.1.) And, specifically:

▷ Among that group, most (46.3%) would choose an organization that is *very* committed — they believe organizations should assume their responsibilities within society — whereas a quarter (24%) would choose an organization with a more modest commitment level, one that would ensure the company's profitability and economic growth.

▷ Fewer than 3% of respondents believe that sustainability is not the role of organizations and would choose their employer accordingly.

_____ Figure 7.1 _____

POSSIBILITY OF CHOOSING YOUR EMPLOYER ACCORDING TO YOUR OWN CRITERIA IN TERMS OF SUSTAINABLE BUSINESS?

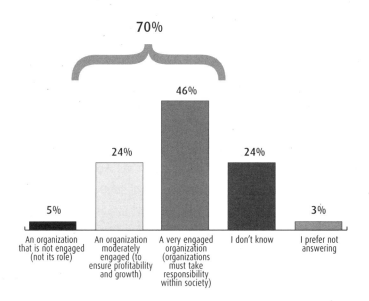

Note: N = 1,502

Answers to this question varied significantly depending on educational levels and employment sectors.

▷ **Education:** The higher the educational level, the greater the expectation for corporate commitment to sustainability. A majority (55.4%) of respondents with a university degree would prefer to be employed by an organization that is very committed to sustainable development.

▷ **Employment sector and size of organization:** Private sector employees who work for big organizations feel quite strongly about the issue: 63.3% of those who work for companies with 1,000–5,000 employees and 60% of those who work for companies with 5,000–10,000 employees would reward the more socially responsible organizations. Likewise, more than two-thirds of employees (67.8%) who work for big government organizations would exercise this specific choice.

With today's shortfall in qualified labour, this data impacts a major human resources issue facing Canadian companies. According to the Conference Board of Canada (2004), "the quality of people and their engagement will be critical factors in corporate vitality and survival." The job market will increasingly favour the candidates, and strategies to seduce and retain qualified workers will intensify over the coming years.

Global Engagement: A New Dominant Definition for Sustainable Development

The survey also tested the ability of respondents to recognize the specific values associated with sustainable development.

Interestingly, the most frequently selected response across Canada was: "global engagement aimed at environmental protection, social well-being, and economic progress." In choosing this answer, two out of five respondents (41%) adequately described sustainable business. (See Table 7.1.)

_____ Table 7.1 _____

RECOGNIZING THE CONCEPT OF SUSTAINABLE DEVELOPMENT

In your opinion, "sustainable business" refers specifically to...

	TOTAL
...global engagement aimed at environmental protection, social well-being, and economic progress.	41%
...environmental protection.	8%
...fair trade products.	7%
...a new trendy concept.	5%
...providing help to developing countries.	1%
None of these choices.	14%
I don't know.	21%
I prefer not answering.	4%

Note: N = 1,502

This percentage jumped significantly for specific occupations, educational levels, employment sectors, and geographic areas:

▷ **Occupation and education:** Approximately half of those who occupy a professional position (49.4%) or have a university degree (54.6%) identified global engagement as the most appropriate definition of sustainable business.[7]

▷ **Employment sector:** The three-dimensional definition ("global engagement aimed at...") was also selected by 46.3% of private sector employees and half (50.7%) of government employees.

▷ **Geographic area:** Of all the Canadian provinces, Quebec had the strongest answers: More than 55% of Quebeckers and 76% of Quebec government employees chose the global engagement definition.

This corroborates the results of another survey of Quebeckers conducted during this same period.[8] Respondents were asked to define sustainable development, and, once again, 55% specifically selected the three-dimensional definition. This second survey also confirms that Quebeckers with a university diploma are more likely to select this definition (62%).

It is likely that the Government of Quebec's *Sustainable Development Act*, which became law in April 2006, and the Government Sustainable Development Strategy that followed in January 2008[9] have contributed to a better understanding of the sustainable development concept on the part of Quebeckers. It will be interesting to monitor the impact that the new federal *Sustainable Development Act*, which became law in June 2008, will have on Canadians across the country.

Fewer Canadians Limit Sustainable Development to Environmental Protection

Only 8.4% of the survey's respondents identified "environmental protection" as the defining criterion for sustainability. This probably reflects a decline in an earlier general tendency to equate sustainable development with environmental protection — until recently, these two notions were regularly regarded as synonymous (Tremblay 2007b), no doubt a consequence of the multiple campaigns deployed since the early 1970s in response to planetary environmental problems.

Organizations Increasingly Under Employee Scrutiny

How are the actions of private companies and other big organizations perceived by their own employees?

Employees seem to be aware of their employers' sustainable development initiatives. More than half (52.5%) of those who work in the Canadian private sector and nearly two-thirds (63.2%) of those who work for a provincial or federal Crown corporation believe that their employers do pay attention to sustainability. Among that group, most (37.5%) considered the level of their employers' commitment to be "moderate"; 20% evaluated it as "moderately high"; and nearly 25% considered their employers to be "industry leaders" in sustainability.

Employees consider sustainability a priority

Do employees consider sustainability to be an important issue? Nearly two-thirds (64%) of respondents who work in the private sector expect their employers to show great interest in sustainability, even making it a priority.

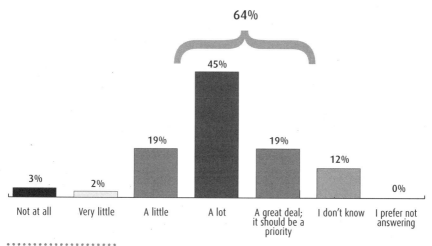

_____ Figure 7.2 _____

IN YOUR OPINION, SHOULD YOUR ORGANIZATION BE INTERESTED IN SUSTAINABILITY?

64%

45%

19%   19%

12%

3%   2%   0%

Not at all   Very little   A little   A lot   A great deal;   I don't know   I prefer not
                                                  it should be a   answering
                                                  priority

Respondents from the private sector

Even more significant, employees who work in organizations with 1,000–5,000 employees and in those with over 10,000 employees (all categories combined) provided this response more than 75% of the time.

Respondents who work in private corporations with over 10,000 employees felt even more strongly — nearly 9 employees out of 10 gave this answer. In addition, more than two-thirds of respondents — those with a university degree (67.6%) and those with an annual income above $80,000 (68.5%) — shared this opinion.

Employees want their employers to walk the talk

Private sector employees remain critical regarding their employers' sincere commitment to global sustainability. Most of them (30.2%) believe that when their employers talk about sustainability, they are primarily focused on business development aimed at economic growth. Another 18% are of the opinion that their employers limit their commitment to making sure the company has a code of conduct and corporate values.

Only 16% of private sector employees believe that their employers interpret sustainability as the development and maintenance of "a global program geared towards protecting the environment, social progress, and economic efficiency."

_____ Table 7.2 _____

PRIVATE SECTOR EMPLOYEES' BELIEFS ABOUT EMPLOYERS
In your opinion, your employer sees its role in sustainable business as...

	TOTAL
...business development aimed at economic growth.	30%
...a code of ethics and organization values.	19%
...a global program geared towards protecting the environment, social progress, and economic efficiency.	16%
...activities to protect the environment.	10%
...donations and community involvement.	4%
None of these choices.	10%
I don't know.	12%
I prefer not answering.	0%

Perceptions die hard. And the perceptions of employees with respect to their employers' public image are worthy of consideration. With a strong proportion of private sector employees who think their employers should be very interested in sustainability, even making it a priority, and where half of them (47%) are able to adequately define the concept of sustainable development, organizations may want to make sure that they close the gap between corporate messaging and concrete action.

Employee communications need to incorporate sustainability messages

More than half (57.6%) of private sector employees feel that they are uninformed or poorly informed by their employers regarding their activities in the sustainability arena.

This data speaks to the still relatively limited space occupied by the communications function within Canadian companies with respect to sustainability issues. A recent study (Tremblay 2006) points out that sustainable development and corporate social responsibility are relatively new themes for corporate communications departments across Canada. In 2004, these topics had not yet found their way onto corporate agendas. By 2006, we were beginning to see an increase in corporate communications on this topic, especially in companies with more than 1,000 employees.

_____ Figure 7.3 _____

DO YOU CONSIDER YOURSELF WELL INFORMED
ABOUT YOUR EMPLOYER'S ACTIVITIES IN THIS REGARD?

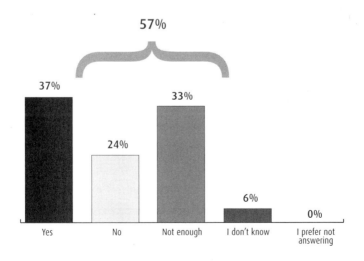

Respondents from the private sector

Participative Values Are Growing

Participative values have grown over the past decade. Citizens feel increasingly concerned and want to be more directly involved in decision making (Inglehart 1990). The survey described on page 180 indicates that 68% of Canadians favour gradual societal change and more direct public participation. In Quebec, more than in the other Canadian provinces, 76% of respondents would like to be directly involved in the process of societal change.

_____ Table 7.3 _____
THREE TYPES OF ATTITUDES TO SOCIETAL CHANGE

	TOTAL – CANADA	TOTAL – QUEBEC
Society must change gradually through various reforms and with the direct participation of citizens.	68%	76%
The way society is organized must change radically.	20%	13%
Society does not need to change.	3%	2%
I don't know.	5%	6%
I prefer not answering.	4%	3%

Note: N = 1,502

It is important to note that participative values are intrinsic to sustainable development, a concept based on bringing parties together — governments, private enterprise, social agents, and civil society — to create an environment that enables all citizens to reach their full potential and improve their quality of life within a society that maintains adequate economic growth. In order to effectively integrate sustainable development values within a given community or organization, there must exist a common vision with respect to the objectives. And the principle of finding solutions that can be shared by the majority must be embraced (Tremblay 2007a). Indeed, sustainable development proposes new forms of partnership by fostering a more consensual social dialogue, new mechanisms for discussion, and greater public participation (Lafferty and Langhelle 1999).

Citizens Send Ever-Clearer Messages to Governments

Citizens also have very precise ideas about what priorities their governments should set. Interestingly, sustainable development values,[10] along with education and economic issues, top the list of priorities with survey respondents across Canada.

Table 7.4
STATEMENTS ABOUT THE ROLE OF GOVERNMENTS
Governments should...

	CANADA – TOTAL AGREE	QUEBEC – TOTAL AGREE
...invest more in education.	81%	86%
...meet current needs without compromising the needs of future generations.	79%	83%
...stimulate the economy.	79%	87%
...implement more effective environmental policies.	78%	89%
...try to limit the negative effects of globalization.	69%	74%
...protect and promote cultural diversity.	61%	65%

Note: N = 1,502

There are, however, significant regional differences. For instance, Quebeckers would like to see the implementation of effective environmental policies while showing concern for the economic situation and investing in education without compromising future generations. Surprisingly, however, the protection and promotion of cultural diversity obtained the lowest score in Quebec, even though this issue was of prime importance during the UNESCO debates, in which Quebec was an active participant (Lachapelle 2008).

The Time for Action Is Now

Because many organizations have, mistakenly, considered the growing interest in sustainable development to be just the latest management trend or they have simply been slow to decode emerging social values, today these same organizations are facing considerable pressure on several fronts. They are finding it difficult or impossible to compete with industry leaders who enjoy positive capital today because they have already embraced sustainable business practices. Their clients are requiring them to respect the standards of accountability that they have adopted for themselves. As if that were not enough, they must deal with the proliferation of media venues, new legislation, and citizens who, more and more, are demanding "ethical" products.

Sustainable development is, of course, not some fad to be followed while it lasts, nor is it a recipe book with a "green" list from which to pluck a few good ideas. In order to build and maintain true corporate social responsibility, organizations cannot rely on the occasional good deed or a cosmetic quick fix.

Organizations face major challenges today: within their walls, a more selective and mobile workforce who is increasingly critical of corporate messaging; outside their walls, a growing constituency of well-informed, assertive citizens who are very conscious of their influence on the world. The data collated across Canada confirms this portrait.

Big organizations must demonstrate a strong capacity to adapt to change in their environment and to translate stakeholder expectations into concrete actions: "To paraphrase Darwin, it is not the powerful organizations that will survive in the new millennium, it is those able to adjust and adapt to a changing world," explain Cutlip, Center, and Broom (2000). An extensive 15-year study conducted in the United States, Canada, and Great Britain shows that, in an increasingly complex environment, high-performance organizations build their communications on constant interaction with their different publics, including interest groups:

> An effective organization exists in an environment characterized more by dynamism and even hostility than by stability. [...] activism pushes organizations toward excellence as they try to cope with the expectations of all their strategic constituencies. [...] Excellent public relations departments scan the environment and continuously bring the voices of publics, especially activist publics, into decision making. Then they develop programs to communicate symmetrically with activists and involve them with managers throughout the organization.
>
> (Grunig, Grunig, and Dozier 2002)

An organization's reputation is increasingly impacted by public trust. Studies show that more and more consumers punish or reward companies for the behaviour and products they condemn or appreciate. In a context where the level of public trust towards big business is very low throughout the world, it has become urgent that certain companies recognize — for the sake of their own viability — that they belong to a social group that is greater than themselves and that they must assume accountability for the social, environmental, and economic impacts created by their activities.

Reputation is a reflection of an organization's actions within the community or with respect to the environment. But it is also based on the quality of the organization's relationship with the new "citizen-consumer." As the political elite and community groups quickly adopted sustainable development values, many corporate citizens began associating the notion of development with the word "sustainable" because they understood that, over and above the quality of their products and services, the ability to stay "top-of-mind" with the consumer also depends on their sense of responsibility and social commitment. Today, the dictates of profit cast a shadow over companies that focus solely on financial results and the shareholder. This is the opinion of the World Business Council for Sustainable Development (WBCSD), an association that includes over 200 multinationals actively involved in sustainable development throughout the world:

> *Pursuing sustainable development makes firms more competitive, more resilient and nimble in a fast-changing world and more likely to win and retain customers. It can also help them find and keep some of the best brains on the market. In addition, it can make them more attractive to investors and insurers, while reducing their exposure to regulatory and other liabilities.*
>
> (WBCSD 2009)

In this light, the communication of organizational performance becomes more of an assessment tool, an element of distinction that confers a competitive edge. For marketing and communications specialists, it now becomes imperative to consider sustainable development as an essential component of public policy and ethical corporate behaviour — a factor that is also measured in the attitudes and behaviour of citizens, voters, and consumers.

REFERENCES

BSR (Business for Social Responsibility). 2009. "About Us: The Business of a Better World." BSR home page, at www.bsr.org/about/index.cfm (accessed 7 May 2009).

Conference Board of Canada. 2004. *Hot HR Issues for the Next Two Years.* Document highlights available online at http://sso.conferenceboard.ca/documents.aspx?did = 1237 (accessed 7 May 2009).

Cutlip, S.M., A.H. Center, and G.M. Broom. 2000. *Effective Public Relations.* 8th ed. Upper Saddle River, NJ: Prentice Hall.

D'Almeida, N. 2007. *La société du jugement: Essai sur les nouveaux pouvoirs de l'opinion.* Paris: Armand Colin.

Drucker, Peter. 1995. *Managing in a Time of Great Change.* New York: Truman Talley Books/Plume.

Grunig, L.A., J.E. Grunig, and D.M. Dozier. 2002. *Excellent Public Relations and Effective Organizations.* Mahwah, NJ: Erlbaum.

Inglehart, I. 1990. *Culture Shift in Advanced Industrial Society.* Princeton, NJ: Princeton University Press.

ISO (International Organization for Standardization). 2008. "Social Responsibility." ISO webpage at www.iso.org/sr. (accessed 6 May 2009).

Lachapelle, G., ed. 2008. *Diversité culturelle, identités et mondialisation: De la ratification à la mise en œuvre de la convention sur la diversité culturelle.* Quebec: Presses de l'Université Laval.

Lafferty, W.M., and O. Langhelle, eds. 1999. *Towards Sustainable Development: On the Goals of Development and the Conditions of Sustainability.* London: Macmillan Press Ltd.

Tremblay, S. 2006. *Développement durable et responsabilités sociales dans la communication d'entreprise: Tendances canadiennes et québécoises (Rapport de recherche).* Chaire en relations publiques, Université du Québec à Montréal.

Tremblay, S. 2007a. "Développement durable et enjeux communicationnels: Les grandes questions," in S. Tremblay, ed. *Développement durable et communications.* Sainte-Foy, QC: Presses de l'Université du Québec.

Tremblay, S., ed. 2007b. *Développement durable et communications: Au-delà des mots, pour un véritable engagement.* Sainte-Foy, QC: Les Presses de l'Université du Québec.

WBCSD (World Business Council for Sustainable Development). 2009. "About the WBCSD: Frequently Asked Questions (FAQs)." WBCSD home page at www.wbcsd.org (accessed 7 May 2009).

WCED (United Nations World Commission on Environment and Development). 1987. *Our Common Future* (Brundtland Report), WCED, April.

CONCLUSION

Overall, we rejected the ingrained notion that clients are disloyal and becoming increasingly so. This gives managers the best excuse for justifying poor performances in terms of sales and business. On the contrary, clients *want* to be loyal and, as we have seen, benefit enormously from remaining loyal. They save time and reduce risks. In fact, loyalty makes their lives easier.

There are numerous examples of companies that default on good customer service. This book even has a Top 10! However, we should not be too quick to cast the first stone, since the competitive context of some business sectors makes it difficult for these companies to fully focus on customer service. Technological innovations have led companies to be continuously fixated on the competition. This is why we suggest that companies adopt a winning management philosophy: *the client before the competition!* It's a question of choice...and of focus.

If it's true that we have been in agreement for the past few decades on the principle of the four P's in marketing (price, place, product, promotion) — that is, orchestrating a coherent marketing strategy to propose an appealing offer to consumers — then, at the same time, we are inviting marketing practitioners to consider the four I's of anti-marketing — (disrespect, inconsistency, indifference, incompetence) — that is, how to avoid consumer dissatisfaction and dislike.

Loyally yours!
Terence Flynn

ABOUT THE AUTHORS

Christian Bourque, *VP, Research, Leger Marketing*

Christian Bourque has 15 years experience in marketing and public opinion research. Before joining Leger Marketing in April 1999, he was senior director of research and spokesperson for the Montreal office of Ipsos Reid (Angus Reid Group at the time). Responsible for media relations, he has frequently been interviewed by *Le Point*, *Le Téléjournal*, *The Journal*, *The National*, *Maclean's*, *USA Today*, the *Globe and Mail*, the *New York Times*, the *Financial Times*, and the *Boston Globe*.

Mr. Bourque is a seasoned moderator (over 1,100 groups) in both English and French, and his quantitative, varied experience has led him to work with clients from the public sector, banking, travel and leisure industries, pharmaceutical companies, professional associations, lotteries, manufacturing, special interest groups, airline carriers, public affairs, communications companies, and advertising agencies.

Along with being a consultant for the firm's senior clients, Mr. Bourque is a keynote speaker at industry events on marketing, communications, and the media. A strong methodologist, he has also been recognized by different courts in Canada as an expert witness on survey research. As such, he has presented survey data to the court and testified on behalf of Leger Marketing.

Mr. Bourque is a member of the Marketing Research and Intelligence Association (MRIA), ESOMAR, and the World Association for Public Opinion Research (WAPOR).

Chuck Chakrapani, *Research Mentor and Industry Liaison Advisor, Ted Rogers School of Management, and Senior Research Fellow, Centre for the Study of Commercial Activity, Ryerson University*

Chuck Chakrapani, PhD, is research mentor and industry liaison advisor at the Ted Rogers School of Management and senior research fellow at the Centre for the Study of Commercial Activity, both at Ryerson University in Toronto. Prior to joining Ryerson, Dr. Chakrapani was the CEO of Millward Brown Canada and held academic appointments at London Business School and the University of Liverpool in England. He currently edits *Marketing Research*, a quarterly publication of the American Marketing Association. He is chief knowledge officer of the Blackstone Group in Chicago, past president of the Professional Marketing Research Society (the forerunner of the MRIA), chairman of the Investors Association of Canada, and a fellow of the Royal Statistical Society.

Guy Lachapelle, *Professor, Department of Political Science, Concordia University*

Dr. Guy Lachapelle has been a professor in the Department of Political Science at Montreal's Concordia University since 1984. He obtained his PhD in Political Science from Chicago's Northwestern University in 1986. Since 2001, he has been the secretary general of the International Political Science Association (IPSA) and was co-chair of the organizing committee for the XVIIIth World Congress of the International Political Science Association in Quebec City (August 1–5, 2000). He has published a number of books, including *Diversité culturelle, identités et mondialisation* (2008); *Claude Ryan et la violence du pouvoir* (2005); *Mastering Globalization: New Sub-states' Governance and Strategies* (with Stéphane Paquin, 2005); *Globalización, Gobernanza E Identidades* (with Francesc Morata and Stéphane Paquin, 2004); *Mondialisation, gouvernance et nouvelle stratégies subétatiques* (with Stéphane Paquin, 2004); *Robert Bourassa: Un bâtisseur tranquille* (with Robert Comeau, 2002); and

Globalization, Governance and Identity (with John E. Trent, 2000). His publications also include contributions to *Revue française de science politique, Publius,* the *Canadian Journal of Political Science, Revue québécoise de science politique, Québec Studies, Canadian Journal of Program Evaluation, Éthique publique,* and *Politique et sociétés.* His views are often sought by the media. His recent work has focused on the impact of globalization, public policy and public opinion theory, and program evaluation.

Serge Lafrance, *VP, Marketing, Leger Marketing*

Holder of a doctoral scholarship in Marketing (University of Montpellier, France) and an MSc in Marketing (Université de Sherbrooke, in Sherbrooke, Quebec), Serge Lafrance is VP, Marketing, at Leger Marketing, the leading Canadian-owned market research and polling firm in Canada. He has acted as a consultant for a number of major companies in the past 15 years, particularly in the areas of retail trade, branding, and corporate reputation management. Moreover, he has developed a superior model of corporate reputation management, the Global Reputation Index (GRI). He has taught several university courses for the EMBA, MBA, and MSc programs, including courses in management, commercial decisions, marketing policies, and international marketing. He has published articles, given lectures, and led seminars in Canada, the US, Chile, Argentina, France, the Netherlands, Luxembourg, Serbia, Portugal, and North and West Africa. He received the award for "Best Paper" from the *Canadian Journal of Marketing Research* in 2006 and was nominated "Best Professor" two years in a row at Université de Sherbrooke (1993 and 1994).

Dimitra Maniatis, *Assistant VP, Leger Marketing, Toronto*

Dimitra Maniatis has been with Leger Marketing since 2006, starting off as a project manager and recently taking on the role of Assistant VP. She has considerable corporate experience, having worked at American Express for a number of years prior to joining Leger Marketing. Ms. Maniatis is an expert on customer satisfaction research and was responsible for all Canadian satisfaction research at American Express. In addition, she sat on a global committee on satisfaction measurement and presented findings and recommendations to senior level executives from Canada, Europe, Japan, Asia Pacific, Australia, and Latin America. Ms. Maniatis is responsible for the overall project administration and design of Leger Marketing research studies, the implementation of questionnaires, the supervision of the data collection process, ensuring the timeliness of deliverables, and the presentation of results and strategic insights/advice. As the customer satisfaction specialist within the organization, she functions as a consultant on all satisfaction studies. Ms. Maniatis has a Bachelor of Commerce, with a major in Management and Enterprise Development and a minor in Law, from Ryerson University. Prior to that, she completed a three-year International Business Administration program at Seneca College in Toronto. She is a member of the MRIA.

Alan C. Middleton, *Executive Director, Schulich Executive Education Centre, Schulich School of Business, York University*

After a stellar 25-year career as a marketing practitioner with Esso and UOP Inc., then rising to the position of executive vice president and board director of J. Walter Thompson (JWT) worldwide and president/CEO of JWT Japan, Dr. Middleton left to complete his PhD at the Schulich School of Business in Toronto where he is currently on the faculty. He has also taught at Rutgers Graduate School of Business in Toronto, in the US and business schools in Argentina, China, Russia, and

Thailand. In September 2001, he took over as executive director of the Schulich Executive Education Centre, which trains over 16,000 managers and executives both domestically and internationally.

Dr. Middleton co-authored the books *Advertising Works II* and *Ikonica: A Fieldguide to Canada's Brandscape* and published papers for the ACA/ICA on marketing communications ROI, client-agency compensation strategies and client-agency relations. He is co-founder of the "Cassie" advertising awards, and in 2005 he was inducted into the Canadian Marketing Hall of Legends in the mentor category.

Douglas Olsen, *Associate Professor, W.P. Carey School of Business, Arizona State University*

Douglas Olsen, BSc, MBA, PhD is an associate professor of Marketing in W.P. Carey School of Business at Arizona State University. Prior to joining ASU, he served as both a professor and the associate dean of MBA programs at the University of Alberta. Dr. Olsen has been active in both graduate and undergraduate programs and teaches marketing strategy, research methodology, consumer behaviour, and marketing communication. His current academic work focuses on factors limiting and enhancing the success of innovation and technology commercialization. Additional work examines factors influencing advertising effectiveness. His academic research has been published in journals that include the *Journal of Advertising, Journal of Advertising Research, Journal of Consumer Research, Journal of Business Research, Journal of Public Policy and Marketing, Journal of Experimental Psychology: Applied, Journal of Consumer Psychology.* He lives in Phoenix with his wife, Lana, and his three sons. During his free time, he enjoys furniture making, painting, and kayaking.

Arancha Pedraz-Delhaes, Project Director, Leger Marketing

Holder of an MSc in Marketing from HEC Montréal, Arancha Pedraz-Delhaes is part of the research team at Leger Marketing's Montreal office, where she works as project director in the realization of marketing research projects, both qualitative and quantitative. She is responsible for managing and coordinating projects, reviewing research tools, reports and other deliverables, as well as preparing strategic conclusions and recommendations. Her dedication to excellence meets clients' expectations and the highest norms of quality. The quality of her work and the success of her mandates are ensured by her concern for efficiency, her spirit of analysis and synthesis, as well as her strategic vision. Ms. Pedraz-Delhaes has collaborated on many large-scale projects and worked for a wide variety of clients, such as Air Canada, the National Bank of Canada, NATIONAL Public Relations, the Canadian Red Cross, Ernst & Young, Europe's Best, FHP, Gaz Métro, Hydro-Québec, Ivanhoe Cambridge, Loto-Québec, Oxford Properties Group, the Société de transport de Montréal, The Brick, and TVA. Brand image management, branding, concept and product testing, customer satisfaction, and advertising are among her fields of interest. Last year, in addition to her work at Leger Marketing, Ms. Pedraz-Delhaes wrote a scientific article in marketing, which she presented at the most recent conference of the prestigious Association for Consumer Research.

Dave Scholz, VP, Leger Marketing, Toronto

Dave Scholz is a partner at Leger Marketing, on Leger's Board of Directors and Vice President responsible for Leger's Toronto office. As well he is a senior consultant to Leger Marketing corporate and Leger International Divisions. With over 15 years experience in public opinion and marketing research, Mr. Scholz has been a leading figure in all phases of both qualitative and quantitative projects across Leger Marketing's divisions.

Mr. Scholz specializes in communication research and holds an M.A. in Cognitive Psychology from the University of Manitoba where he completed his Master thesis on the effects of Reading on Attitudinal Measures. In the past few years, he has developed a Reputation Measurement Index for Leger Marketing and has published an annual report on corporate reputation in Canada for the past four years. His experience in reputation research has led him to be a keynote speaker on reputation and risk management research at various international conferences.

Dave is also an adjunct professor at McMaster University and Syracuse University's joint Masters in Communication program and teaches a course on Public Relations Research. He also guest lectures at many graduate and undergraduate programs.

Sylvain Sénécal, Associate Professor, HEC Montréal

Associate professor at HEC Montréal since 2004 and chairholder of the RBC Financial Group Chair of Electronic Commerce since September 2007, Sylvain Sénécal holds a PhD in Business Administration from HEC Montréal. His research has been presented at many international conferences and published in journals such as *Journal of Retailing* and *International Journal of Electronic Commerce*. In addition to his teaching experience in the US, he has provided training for international companies such as MittalSteel and Doosan.

Solange Tremblay, MA, *Université du Québec à Montréal*

Solange Tremblay is an Associate Professor in the Department of Social and Public Communication and a founding member of the Chair in Public Relations and Marketing Communication at UQAM. She is also Director of the Centre for Sustainable Development, Ethics and Communications, a research group studying communications issues in sustainable development and social responsibility, as well as ethical questions in communication practice. She is the lead author of *Développement durable et communications: Au-delà des mots, pour un véritable engagement* (Presses de l'Université du Québec, 2007). Her participation in numerous research studies in the field of communications, public relations, corporate responsibility, and sustainable development gives her a unique insight into the challenges faced by today's communicators. In addition, she has more than 20 years of professional experience in communications and is a frequent contributor to industry forums and publications.

NOTES

1   This is an obvious oversimplification. Many customers stay with the same company for several other reasons, such as the costs associated with the switch and its attendant inconvenience or simple inertia. In addition, if a company consistently follows market norms, its businesslike approach can create consumer trust and thereby create loyalty. However, for the time being we will ignore these for the purposes of understanding the nature of market and social norms.

2   The term "dashboard" is explained on page 49. The balanced scorecard, in recognition of the fact that financial information is not the only measurement of an organization's progress, consists of four equal and interlinked measures of progress: financial, customer, business processes and learning, and growth. With measures in each of these areas, the progress of an organization can be better understood. The customer measures include measures of customer segments in areas such as share, customer retention, new customer acquisition, customer satisfaction, and customer profitability and, as such, are measures built into marketing dashboard measures.

3   Those who are unfamiliar with the term "share of wallet" can consult the explanation on page 49.

4   "Conative" is a fairly recent word, used largely in psychological discourse. *Merriam-Webster's Online Dictionary* defines it as "an inclination (as an instinct, a drive, a wish, or a craving) to act purposefully," and *The Free Dictionary* online defines it as and "the aspect of mental processes or behavior directed toward action or change including impulse, desire, volition, and striving." Conation, then, is associated with more commonly understood words, such as "motivation," "will," and "drive."

5   The question (not exact wording) asks respondents to choose between three options: (1) more reasons to keep their current brand versus switching, (2) as many good reasons to stay with their current brand or switch, and (3) more reasons to switch than keep their current brand.

6   The term "dashboard" is explained on page 49.

7   The survey does, however, show a lack of awareness on the part of homemakers: Nearly half (46.9%) admit not knowing what "sustainable development" means.

8   This refers to a Leger Marketing survey of 1,000 Quebeckers conducted between July 30 and August 3, 2008.

9 In the wake of Quebec's *Sustainable Development Act*, the implementation of Quebec's 2008–2013 Government Sustainable Development Strategy has been part of a vast plan to raise awareness, educate, and provide training. Since January 2008, the 150 Quebec government departments, agencies, and Crown corporations have worked to implement the law's objectives. Citizens and corporations alike will be increasingly encouraged to fall into step and adopt practices that contribute to these sustainable development goals.

10 Universal definition: "Sustainable development is development that meets the needs of the present without compromising the ability of future generations to meet their own needs." (WCED 1987)

Faites-nous part
de vos commentaires

Assurer la qualité de nos publications
est notre préoccupation numéro un.

N'hésitez pas à nous faire part de
vos commentaires et suggestions
ou à nous signaler toute erreur
ou omission en nous écrivant à :

livre@transcontinental.ca

Merci !

Les Éditions
Transcontinental